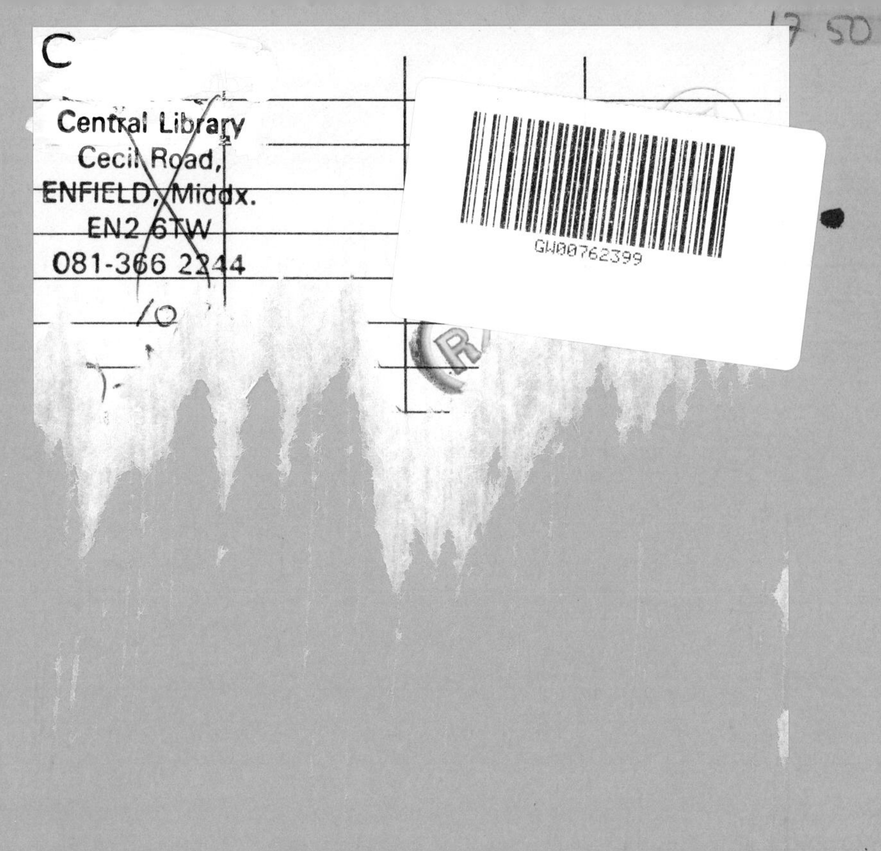

Language and Rhetoric of the Revolution

Language and Rhetoric of the Revolution

edited by
John Renwick
and
produced with the assistance of the
Institut Français d'Ecosse
Edinburgh

EDINBURGH UNIVERSITY PRESS

22 George Square, Edinburgh

Set in Linotron Garamond 3
by Koinonia, Bury, and
printed in Great Britain by
Redwood Press Limited,
Trowbridge, Wilts

British Library Cataloguing
in Publication Data
Language and rhetoric of the Revolution.
I. Renwick, John, *1939*–
944.041014
ISBN 0 7486 0122 8

CONTENTS

NOTES ON CONTRIBUTORS

Peter FRANCE, sometime Fellow of Magdalen College, Oxford and Reader at the University of Sussex (1962–1980) has been Professor of French at the University of Edinburgh since 1980. He has published numerous books and articles on the seventeenth and eighteenth centuries, in particular: *Racine's Rhetoric* (1965); *Rhetoric and Truth in France: Descartes to Diderot* (1972); *Diderot* (1983) and *Rousseau: Confessions* (1987). Peter France is a Fellow of the British Academy.

Lynn HUNT is former Professor of History at the University of California, Berkeley, and Fellow of the Institute for Advanced Study, Princeton (1988–1989). She is currently Joe and Emily Lowe Foundation Term Professor in the Humanities at the University of Pennsylvania and is the author of the acclaimed study: *Politics, Culture, and Class in the French Revolution* (1984).

John RENWICK, sometime Fellow of Churchill College, Cambridge, Maître de conférences at the University of Clermont (1970–1974) and then Professor of French in the New University of Ulster, has been Professor of French at the University of Edinburgh since 1980. He has published extensively on the literary and cultural history of the eighteenth century and is the author of *Marmontel* (1972); *Marmontel, Voltaire and the* Bélisaire *affair* (1974); *Voltaire et Morangiés* (1982) and *Chamfort devant la postérité* (1986).

Philippe ROGER was Associate Professor at New York University (1978-1985) and is now Chargé de recherche at the CNRS. He is the author of

Sade. La philosophie dans le pressoir (1976) and of *Roland Barthes, roman* (1986). He edited the proceedings of the Cerisey colloquium devoted to Sade (*Sade: écrire la crise,* 1980) and has contributed to various collective works, the most recent being *La Mort de Marat* (1986).

Eric WALTER, Maître de conférences at the University of Picardy (Amiens), is an eighteenth-century specialist with wide-ranging interests in literature, history and politics. He has published on Diderot, Voltaire, the Revolution, and the book trade in Picardy; he has contributed to the *Histoire de l'édition française* (1984) and to the *Lieux de mémoire, I. La République* (1984) as also to *La Mort de Marat*.

PREFACE

The present volume, containing the proceedings of a colloquium jointly mounted on 11–12 April 1989 by the Institut Français d'Ecosse and the French Department of the University of Edinburgh, has been prepared with the help and cooperation of a large number of people. I am conscious of my debt to Alain Bourdon, Director of the Institut Français, who with his own colleagues worked so hard to organise the colloquium and who has so generously helped to finance the publication of our proceedings which appropriately, in this year of the *bicentenaire*, took place in an atmosphere of liberty and equality, but above all of international fraternity. I am equally grateful to Professor Denis Roberts, Librarian of the National Library of Scotland, who drew material from the Crawford Collection of Revolutionary documents and who mounted, uniquely for the benefit and pleasure of the participants in the colloquium, an exhibition which he invited them to enjoy in elegant and festive surroundings.

I wish to acknowledge the grant which the administrators of the University of Edinburgh Faculty of Arts Research Fund so readily made towards the material preparation of this volume. My thanks are due also to the French Department's two secretaries, Tessa Brown and Deborah McVittie, who worked uncomplainingly within a timetable which necessarily had to be demanding if our publication were to figure as a timely contribution towards the celebration of 1789. Against an unavoidable background of constant minor crisis, (due essentially to that race against time), Martin Spencer and Vivian Bone of the University Press invariably responded with advice, encouragement and understanding. I am most grateful to them both.

Above all, I wish to express my gratitude to my colleague Peter France whose ready advice over these last two months has been invaluable.

JOHN RENWICK

Edinburgh, 15 June 1989

ACKNOWLEDGEMENTS

Permission to reproduce the illustrations is gratefully acknowledged to the following:

Figure 1. Musée du Louvre, Paris.
Figure 2. Bibliothèque Nationale, Paris. (Photo B.N.)
Figure 3. Bibliothèque Nationale, Paris. (Photo B.N.)
Figure 4. Bibliothèque Nationale, Paris. (Photo B.N.)
Figure 5. Musée Carnavalet, Paris. (Photo Lynn Hunt.)
Figure 6. Musée Calvet, Avignon. (Photo Musée Calvet.)

One

INTRODUCTION

John Renwick

When the French Revolution broke, it became quickly evident that this was indeed going to be a revolution which meant upheaval and a wholesale redefinition of institutions. For it was clear from the start that the Revolutionaries, engaged in a deeply political event, wished to mark themselves off absolutely from the preceding regime (which was soon referred to in France – with remarkable linguistic prescience – as the *former* regime). In the ensuing comprehensive reform of institutions (and language pre-1789 had been considered an institution like any other), it was unavoidable that language itself as both the marker of, and the vehicle for, political change should attract the keen attention of the Revolutionaries. But first – though not without bitter opposition – it had to be liberated and adapted to the task in hand. In a very real sense it was initially unequal to that task: whereas various languages, various types of rhetoric and eloquence had been recognised and encouraged by the monarchy (for example, the bar, the pulpit and the Academies), that language and that eloquence which could have been 'liberatory' – in other words: the political – had been either banned or strongly discouraged. This is not to say that France had been ignorant of a political language and a political discourse of sorts; but more often than not they had existed in forms that 'dared not speak their name' (romances, didactic or pedagogical novels, plays, history, Ancient and Modern; art criticism... even archaeology and anthropology). Where it did exist as such, it was either well- controlled, sanitised or used by the 'Establishment' in pursuance of its own ends, failing which it was an (illegally produced) vehicle for dissent, for criticism, for the expression of disgust which, not surprisingly, tended to be scurrilous or negative. Now, with new hands on the controls, language – once duly modernised and made equal to the great tasks ahead – was seen (whether as sign or symbol) as being the Revolutionaries' indispensable vehicle for ensuring their own liberation and guiding their own destinies through totally uncharted territory. This is the time when that word and the concrete reality that it transmitted (or the dreams that it purveyed) could be exhilarating and inspirational, or sombre and baleful. As Michelet once said, writing about this problem and this period: 'There were words that saved and words that killed'. That is the precise measure of the power and importance of language under the Revolution.

The central focus of this collection of papers and round-table discussions is the language and rhetoric of the period 1789–1797. The papers themselves, covering areas that the four internationally acknowledged specialists in the field themselves considered to be particularly significant, deal with problems that are apparently diverse: logomachy; the imagery of the *affective* base of power; the rhetorical performance of deputies in the newly-elected Convention; Babeuf's projection of himself through language. Diverse though they may appear to be, they are however remarkably convergent. The index alone will show that a large corpus of topics and problems occur with regularity from one paper to the next, one round-table discussion to the other: the essential considerations concerning language, rhetoric and discourse cut across them all – or rather *unite* them all – with a frequency that is illuminating. The papers and their resultant round-tables necessarily produced many more hours of recorded proceedings and debate than could conveniently be reproduced within a volume of strictly prescribed length. In one sense therefore (but this is an ironic illustration of that oft-repeated truism which is only too well- known to all who are interested in language and rhetoric), the round-table discussions themselves, as printed, can convey only in the most inadequate fashion the feelings of sheer excitement and enthusiasm which were generated by the confrontation and exchange of views.(Perhaps – like the journalists of the *Moniteur* reporting on the daily business of the National Assembly – I should have added appropriate 'stage-directions': *double salve d'applaudissements; murmures d'approbation; plusieurs colloquants se précipitent à la tribune...*). But needless to say, a 'recreation' of the atmosphere in Randolph Crescent could have been achieved (and even then as a mere echo) only through integral verbatim reproduction of some ten hours of recording in both English and French. Such a solution, for a whole variety of reasons – which *habitués* of conferences will not find difficult to discern – would have been materially onerous not to say (above all) aesthetically detestable. Editorial intervention has therefore been unavoidable. Whenever possible I have, however, scrupulously respected the authentic voice of each individual *intervenant* and – where this has been beyond me – respected nevertheless the spirit if not the (disjointed, fractured or leisurely) letter of what they said.

For the sake of uniformity, all contributions originally produced in French, whether papers or debate, have been rendered into English. Where appropriate I have, however, judged it advisable to give the reader a flavour of the original without ever losing from sight that reader for whom French is not a natural medium of communication.

Two

THE FRENCH REVOLUTION AS 'LOGOMACHY'

Philippe Roger

If there are two ways of looking at the French Revolution which are scorned by modern historiography, it is those that were adopted by La Harpe and Louis-Sébastien Mercier. The fact is, the historian sees it as a great mistake on the part of a historical figure to have *lived* through the times which he personally is endeavouring to reconstruct. It is an even greater mistake to have *played a role* in them. Although there is no need to set about rehabilitating the two men in question (this would in any case be paradoxical if it were to lump together La Harpe, the new convert to religion and Mercier, the undaunted republican) it does seem that a new look at them both would be appropriate. One argument at least for that new look would be quite enough to intrigue the historian: both men – in considering the Revolution – share one and the same (though a differently used) scheme of explanation. They both have recourse (though in ideologically divergent discourses) to one and the same topos, that of a language which has been degraded, debased or, more pointedly – to take a word used by both – which has been *desecrated*. As a preamble, it would be useful to compare these two witnesses who were initially keen participants in a Revolution against which, after 1795, they will give evidence and pass judgement.

La Harpe, it has been said, abjures the Revolution and *Philosophy* and resurrects the altars of that very religion which he had helped to overthrow. He is to be counted among those pious penitents whom Sade rebaptises as 'la tourbe dévotieuse' (the devotious horde).[1] On the other hand, Louis-Sébastien Mercier, who was close to the Girondins, who was a member of the the Convention but not a regicide, and who came through the Terror but did not renege on the Republic, kept faith with a certain idea of the grandeur of the popular movement (which will appear to him to be Bonaparte's inheritance). La Harpe has above all been read in the light of Bonald and De Maistre, whereas Mercier has been read in the light of the Girondins. But *both* were fascinated by language. And that fascination contributed in no small measure to the way in which they read the Revolution. If their respective analyses of the 'language of the Revolutionaries' are of interest to us here, it is because – in spite of fundamentally different political choices and epistemological presuppositions – their analyses are remarkably convergent in that they see the essence of the revolutionary phenomenon in the rape of language and its apparent referentiality.

La Harpe's turnabout comes as early as 1794 and the violence of that turnabout is betrayed by the title of the speech he gave on 31 December to mark the opening of the Lycée: *De la guerre declarée par les tyrans révolutionnaires à la raison, à la morale, aux lettres et aux arts*. Already the language question is posed. Too vast, however, to be dealt with in the context of his lecture, it is kept for a future detailed study which La Harpe announces as follows: 'My examination of the words themselves will necessarily lead me to an examination of all the things which were done with words'.[2] That examination will, in 1797, be his: *Du Fanatisme dans la langue révolutionnaire ou de la Persécution exercée par les barbares du XVIIIe siècle contre les ministres de la religion chrétienne*. This particular text is too wide-ranging to be analysed in detail here; its thrust, however, is in showing that the 'language of the Revolutionaries'had been the lever used to subvert institutions and to bring about the recent social upheaval. What, according to La Harpe, is that 'language of the Revolutionaries'? It is a distinct linguistic corpus, a sub-species existing within the French language and yet one which had been substituted by guile or by force for the latter: an 'intolerable jargon substituted for the French language'.[3]

To the potential universality of the latter, La Harpe opposes the particularism which he sees in the former; and indeed as he gets deeper into his text the linguistic dimension of that 'language of the Revolutionaries' visibly shrinks. Initially the language of the Revolution, it soon becomes the language of a mere fraction of the people then, finally, of a faction usurping the status of the people. Apostrophising the supporters of the Revolution in his speech of 1794, La Harpe had already branded that language as the language of the '300,000 bandits whom you called the people'.[4] But now, ever contracting, that language has become a mere jargon, worse still an argot. It is the jargon of the Jacobins (whom La Harpe designates by the capitalised word: LA FACTION) and whom he addresses in these rough terms: 'when will you realise then that all the fanciful epithets that went to construct your vile jargon get no further than your papers and your clubs, in the same way as thieves' cant does not spread beyond their caverns'.[5]

This new myth of the cavern deserves a word or two. For far from being confined to dens and thieves' kitchens, as La Harpe would have it, the 'language of the Revolutionaries' makes, in 1798, a resounding appearance in the *Dictionnaire*, and not just any dictionary, but that of the French Academy! In that year an Appendix to it sets out, astonishingly, to list those newly minted words which had been spawned by the Revolution: there are 418 of them. Such at least is the verdict arrived at by the faceless *hommes de lettres* who had undertaken the task. Who were they? The preface tells us that they 'did not wish to be named'.[6] Evidently those who are putting the seal of approval on this revolutionary vocabulary are themselves linguistically uneasy: what if they were to be seen as the celebrants of that cult, now receding into the past, but part of whose ritual they are now recording? For here they are, setting down – from the arid glossary of that new administration (that same glossary does not however appear 'innocent' to its enemies, and Burke saw the anarchist plot starting with the word *département*), here they are then setting down and giving semantic respectability to the neologisms of terror: *carmagnole, cordeliers, enragé, fournée, lanterne, noyades*, and even *septembriser, septembrisade* – along with this example: *Une telle fut sept...ée à la Force.* There is something both heroic and pathetic about this insistence on the part of the recently resurrected Academy that it can 'give laws' that nobody however dares countersign. 'My answer is that a good *Dictionnaire* can alone give to a nation those laws of speech which are perhaps more important than the very laws of social organisation',[7] says the intrepid preface-writer; but neither he nor his colleagues, logothetes of the revolutionary lexicon, are at pains to claim paternity for their 'important' work.

Whatever the case may have been for La Harpe, he himself saw the 'language of the Revolutionaries' as a language which was barbarous in both senses of the word: for him barbarism and barbarity were inextricably bound up in it. In his eyes, Fouquier-Tinville the neologist and ignoramus is inseparable from Fouquier-Tinville the purveyor to the Guillotine. Rather than give a gloss on his 'crimes', La Harpe recalls one of his mixed metaphors: 'to sow disorganisation'. What is his final word on the ex-Public Prosecutor? 'He cared little for the accuracy of figures'.[8] Those are economical words of abuse. And that remarkable understatement subsumes all other criticisms. . . .

The 'language of the Revolutionaries' is thus reduced by La Harpe to being a mere trifle: a handful of 'abuse as meaningless as it was violent'. And yet it was that language itself which had caused the Revolution and which 'had been its first instrument and the most surprising instrument of them all'.This is a paradox which La Harpe can describe only as a decree of Providence: 'the establishment and legal consecration' of that language is 'a unique event, an unprecedented scandal in human history, which remains totally inexplicable except in terms of divine retribution'.[9] This is the beginning of an astonishing reversal on the part of the author. What had seemed condemned to being insignificant now becomes a Power as much as a Sign; the initial abuse turns upside-down and becomes head-spinning fascination: unique, unprecedented, totally inexplicable, the most surprising instrument of them all. . . It is the 'language of the Revolutionaries' which lies at the heart of the Great Secret; it is the last word of that Revolution as it had been 'its first instrument'. *Du fanatisme dans la langue révolutionnaire* could (and should) have been entitled the 'Apocalypse according to La Harpe': it is the unveiling of a revolutionary Mystery which is one with the Mystery of its 'inverse language'. But the analysis peters out, the revelation remains hidden. Instead, we find – in a note – this strange exclamation, this admission which destroys the whole critical and demonstrative purpose behind the book: 'Yes but! you have not been initiated into the secrets of that language; it is a powerful system of symbols, although I cannot as yet give you the dictionary for it'.[10] He will never do so.

Mercier, for his part, will produce in 1801 that work of anticipatory terminology which he entitled *Néologie*; but it will be *his* dictionary and not that of the Revolution. He himself warns his reader that, 'with a few exceptions', he has 'ommitted those words which directly concern the Revolution'.[11] At the end of the strange preface which stands at the head of *Néologie*, Mercier reproduces his own version of La Harpe's procrastination. Speaking to, and about, the Nation, he writes: 'I could soon reproduce before its eyes and bring back to its ears the virile expressions of that republican language which I knew so well for four or five years. There you'ld find something to make monarchical language turn pale for ever'.[12] This 'republican language', which is a language that is already dead but which can be restored and which is remembered proudly by Mercier, is not only the opponent of the 'language of the Court', but is also the antidote for the 'empty, hollow language' of the Terror and of Jacobinism. On the latter, and despite the gulf which, after 1794, has opened up between them both politically speaking, Mercier expresses himself in a way which is remarkably similar to that of La Harpe. The essential text in this respect is the preface to his *Nouveau Paris* (1798) in which he analyses the role played by language in the revolutionary event and in which, at the same time, he calculates the possibility of inventing an idiom capable of expressing 'so many barbaric sights', in other words: capable of writing the Revolution . . . so as to interpret it. Here you find more or less the same attacks that La Harpe himself had directed at the 'language of the Revolutionaries', i.e. abuse of words and malicious alteration of their meaning. Here you can also sense a similar horror at the 'dreadful chaos created by the writers of the Revolution' and their 'enormous mass of newssheets'.[13] Here also you can see the same paradoxical coupling of emptiness-hollowness and mortal danger: 'Calling people names abusively, that is to say using words that had no sense, that was to pass sentence of death', and again :'It was all those empty, hollow phrases, and even those which were the most unintelligible, which were what bound the prisons and the scaffolds together'.[14] Here you can also find the same denunciation of a plot against the language; here 'LA FACTION' becomes 'the ambitious demagogic horde' which 'created for itself a language calculated to deceive and seduce the multitude' ('sublime heights of extravagance'), which was however 'understood' and which 'did succeed'.[15] This is a passage which Mercier concludes with the following final exclamation: 'and we, should *we* not create a language in order to transmit to the last of our line those incredible moral and political phenomena?' The neology which is invoked here is definitely the reply of the educated man and citizen to that warped form of speech which had subjugated the *classes populacières* (base-born classes). It is the revenge of the Arts, or of the *Philosophes-Artistes*, over those who only think to *délibérer par bras* (debate with their fists). We are no longer dealing with the barbarians of La Harpe, but with savages.

Although everything should separate a Mercier (who, in 1798, still does not regret having called, in 1789, for the destruction of the Château de Versailles) from someone like La Harpe (who is given to fits of rage that would suit a political flagellant), it is nevertheless clear that the *instituteur national* (tutor to the nation) and the Professor at the Lycée are – in their respective denunciations of the 'language of the Revolutionaries' – following paths which are remarkably similar. Mercier, who is unabashed, who refuses to recant openly and to incriminate the Revolution *en bloc* as an insult to Church and Throne in equal measure, hits however upon the same strongly charged word, i.e *desecrated*, which is used by La Harpe to convey the affront that had been done the language by the Revolution gone astray : 'It is perhaps because we have desecrated the language that we have lost some of our virtues'.[16]

This convergence is significant. It is significant in exactly the same way as the anonymity which had been carefully preserved by the authors of the Appendix to the *Dictionnaire* of the Academy is significant, and whose ambiguous behaviour raises the question of the 'language of the Revolutionaries' as being a special language, a burning language, an inascribable language, and which was however a language which cannot be skirted round, an ineffaceable language even though it forces those who enumerate its vocabulary to efface *themselves*. The question of the 'language of the Revolutionaries' seen from this angle, is not a matter for lexicography even if the innovation was lexical in kind. It is political, philosophical, and religious too. For if that 'language of the Revolutionaries' is denounced by its detractors as being intrinsically sacrilegious, it will increasingly be extolled by the opposing camp as pure Energy and Power of the Word.

Seen from the post-thermidorian vantage point, through these still impassioned but already reflective texts, the Revolution comes to us in the unusual guise of a war of words. But this particular feeling about the language which is shared by La Harpe and Mercier does not apparently derive from a retrospective illusion or a 'professional quirk'. There is no doubt that the Revolution was interpreted and lived, from 1789 onwards, by its detractors but also by its supporters, as a 'logomachy'. In this sense, we must reformulate the problem of the 'language of the Revolutionaries' to make it the problem of a political struggle around the language, which is conducted through the language itself and which appeals to ('modern', enlightened) linguistic science and an (archaic) mythology of the powers of the Word. From 1789 on there is an open war for control of the language. The revolutionary ranks themselves are divided by it. But it was not the revolutionaries who declared that war: the lexical guerilla campaign launched in 1789 by the counter- revolutionary pamphleteers predates the dream of a 'revolutionised' French and sheds light on it.

The battle called for a common battleground, a common epistemological field upon which the adversaries could meet. This ground or this field is none other than the incessantly repeated and exalted topos of the 'empire of words'. The formula is universal, omnipresent. It punctuates and justifies the reforming conclaves of Urbain Domergue's 'Société délibérante des amateurs de la langue française'. Talleyrand in turn puts his voice and his authority behind this notion in his *Rapport sur l'Instruction publique* (10 September 1791), which is a thorough-going dissertation on language presented for the meditation of the 'Assemblée nationale which is, of course, acquainted with the power of the word, and which knows how much influence, or rather effect, signs have on ideas and through them on the habits which it wishes to create or to consolidate'.[17] But this formula reappears just as often in monarchist writings: Gallais shares the same belief when he states: 'Words, grand words impress children of all ages'.[18] He is not the only one on his side of the house to think so. 'We are acquainted with the power of signs', writes the equally royalist Buée in 1792. 'It is signs which, bringing to our minds grand, strong, sublime ideas, raise us up above ourselves'.[19] That way of putting things would not be repudiated by the patriotic Abbé Grégoire who, in turn, at about the same time, and at the rostrum of the Convention, ponders the semantic lessons of history: 'History testifies that, in all centuries, we see, on the one hand, peoples quarrelling and slaughtering one another on account of words and, on the other hand, words giving birth to heroic deeds'.[20]

Whether we look at the 'aristocratic' pamphleteer or the democratic publicist or the democratic deputy, we find the same religion of the sign. That consensus comes from a certain epistemology, the theoretical base of which lies in the concept of language as representation. If the word is there *to represent* the idea of the thing, any disturbance in the realm of vocabulary reflects or foreshadows a disorder in the realm of mental representations. So we can move from the representative sign to the idea, and from the idea to its object with rapidity: the buffer of the Saussurian 'referent' has yet to be invented. For the polemicists of 1789–92, few of whom moreover are true 'grammarians', that to-and-fro movement between words and things looks very much like a short-circuit. Each lexicological skirmish is thought to project them into the heart of reality in exactly the same way as each revolutionary 'novelty' (of that they are quite sure) cannot fail to disturb the language. 'Languages always feel the effects of any and every revolution, in opinions, in mores, and above all in governments', writes the 'independent' Suard in 1791.[21] And Grégoire adds in turn:'the philosopher knows that names have a great impact on things; that, according to their nature, they serve as a magnet for patriotism, for virtues, for errors, for factions'.[22] The shift from things to words, but also from words to things, is a perpetual current whose toing-and-froing charges Reality and Language by turns. This common conviction animates counter-revolutionary lampoons and Jacobin decrees alike; both emanate from an epistemology of representation whose 'natural' result is a shared belief in the dangerous powers of language. Some may be aristocrats, others democrats, but *all* are semiocrats.

It is in this context that, as early as 1789, there begins a struggle for control of the language: a logomachy breaks out over a Revolution which is itself qualified as a 'logomachy' by its protagonists. For the grammarians do not monopolise this politico-linguistic awareness. Far from its being the prerogative of the partisans of the Revolution, it can be seen finding expression, very early on, in one of the most unexpected of 'speakers': Louis XVI in person. This King with his inconsistent behaviour which was so often so 'impolitic', this King whom even his own followers called a 'sot' (a fool, a noodle) [23] is however the first person to speak out – with remarkable lucidity – against the insidious onward march of the opposing vocabulary, the first to stigmatise – in political terms – the use of neologism in which he sees the Trojan Horse of all attacks on power. He does so publicly, solemnly, in his letter of 16 June 1789 to the Third Estate, in two little sentences which ran: 'Je désapprouve l'expression répétée des classes privilégiées que le tiers état emploie. . . Ces expressions inusitées ne sont propres qu'à entretenir un esprit de division' (I disapprove of the repeated use of the expression *privileged classes* that the Third Estate is using. . . These novel expressions are good only to perpetuate a spirit of divisiveness.)[24] That was how Louis XVI laid bare the inherently 'revolutionary' nature of a lexical invasion which was, even at this early date, an attack on institutions. Identifying the Third Estate as the source of these unwanted signs, he questioned the right of one particular social group to legislate on the vocabulary, and at the same time implicitly denounced the clear pretention of that group to be *the totality*, which is what Sièyes – in his famous pamphlet – had just claimed on its behalf. That was how, a decade earlier than La Harpe, Louis XVI launched the theme of the 'language of the part' which seeks to take over the 'language of the whole'. But not content with pointing to the political stakes in this neological offensive ('these novel expressions'), he also drew attention in passing to the method used. Speaking of 'repeated use', he hinted at that mechanism of constant repetition, that constant drumming on people's minds with revolutionary neology. This was a commonplace which was in turn to prove immensely productive, starting with the *Extrait d'un Dictionnaire inutile* of the Royalist Gallais and going down to the *Nouveau Paris* of Louis-Sébastien Mercier.

It is very difficult to judge what impetus the King's intervention imparted. Did it in fact lead to the (variable) verve of the Royalists who – during the coming months – were to take up the same gauntlet? Someone like Espréménil is probably echoing the King's intervention when he 'observed' at the rostrum, in February 1791, 'that one of the means familiarly used in this assembly to lead our thoughts astray is the continual use of new expressions'.[25] But that is not the real point: the fact is that, by making vocabulary into a privileged form of the counter-revolutionary lampoon, the (often anonymous) pamphleteers of the years 1789–92, faced with the dislocators of vocabulary, betray the same concern as their King did. They all embark upon a campaign to deal with the attacks made on the language, attacks which are detrimental to the political order: to their way of thinking, the body of the King, the social body, the body of the language, constitute a continuum which is exposed to one and the same threat.

At first sight, the political dictionaries and glossaries which appeared during the period 1789–92 are hardly of a piece, either in size (one will 'explain' two words, whereas another will 'explain' two hundred) or in style: alongside genuine pamphlets, you can find certain publications which, in the main, set out to reproduce decrees of the Assembly and articles of the Constitution. All, however, share the same lay-out which is that of the (generally alphabetical) list that comprises a very variable number of headed entries. Imbued with political ideology, full of 'collected' neo- logisms, such is the nature and configuration of these dictionaries which are not only a privileged 'source' of information about people's thoughts on the language, but which also delineate a history which is the history of the Revolution as a struggle between modes of speech. For these dictionaries follow one another, know, answer, correct, denounce and insult one another. They are – from the most apparently staid to the most openly injurious – machines of war.

The first surprise, upon examining these productions of the years 1789–92, comes when we see that it is not the spokesmen for the Revolution who open the hostilities. The glossaries favourable to the Revolution are rare and, above all, are not very aggressive. In a word, they are less absent than *distant*. On the opposing side, however, there is an immediate fondness for this type of political vehicle which gets its adaptability from the dictionary form and its virulence from the pamphlet. What are they fighting against? Against men (Mirabeau, La Fayette), against ideas (national sovereignty, liberty of the press) but also, and above all, against the first linguistic innovations that the summer of 1789 puts into 'every mouth'. The counter-revolutionary dictionaries – with their vigorous approach and their harsh tone – set their faces against this living word which is both elusive and protean, and whose effervescence characterises the early phase of the Revolution. The Jacobin counter-offensive will come later, as though the 'revolutionarisation of the language' had had to be prefaced by a sort of aristocratic reaction that was linguistic in character.

The originality of this corpus resides less in its themes than in the form that people chose to give it: to have recourse to the dictionary-form is immediately to suggest the essentially linguistic nature of the revolutionary event itself. The favour enjoyed by the glossary in the ranks of the early counter-revolution betrays the sheer intensity of that conviction which sees the Revolution as being, above all, a *misunderstanding*. It is the notion of a misunderstanding – before the theme of the conspiracy comes into its own – which provides a theoretical explanation for an upheaval which is incomprehensible and unjustifiable. The revolutionary situation is experienced by these pamphleteers as being, inseparably, social disorder and interference with meanings. And it is the latter which makes the former possible. In this situation, the literary 'form' you choose and the political analysis you give are also inseparable: both fuse together in one and the same approach which is dictated by the crying need to counter-attack on the lexical terrain, and to counter-attack to the precise extent that the country's troubles begin and grow against a background of cacophony.

There is no longer any mutual understanding, and it is the semantic confusion itself which engenders or furthers that 'division' which Louis XVI deplored in those early days. So much is universally acknowledged. Such is the constant premise of the dictionaries: 'we do not understand one another, and. . . what is more, very often we do not understand ourselves'. That affirmation is to be found at the beginning of the *Avis à mes chers concitoyens sur les querelles d'allemand, ou Discours sur les noms de parti qu'on se donne réciproquement sans vouloir s'entendre*. The title alone proverbially[26] identifies the revolutionary event with a stupid quarrel, a pointless quarrel (Littré).

What gives the counter-revolutionary dictionaries their momentum is, first, the conviction that the monarchical cause has to be defended on the battlefield of words. Next, it is the certainty that their interpretation of words is right. In the light of the evidence their violence – they believe – is permissible, and it is to the old criteria of clarity and distinctness that they appeal when they are faced with the excesses of their adversaries. Recourse to the dictionary-form is calculated as the means of holding back that flood of 'meaningless phrases', as a means of restoring a stable and defined world. The Abbé Morellet, who could give some hard knocks, the man who set about Domergue in Year IV, will quite simply entitle his lexical, anti-Jacobin column in the *Mercure de France*: 'Le Définisseur' ('The Definer'). A definition is the buffer up against which the verbal excess, the intemperance and the fraud of the revolutionary word will come to grief. Hence, the case against 'abuse of words', previously made by the philosophical tradition, from Bacon, Locke, Hobbes and Spinoza down to Helvétius, D'Alembert and Diderot finds its new public prosecutors among the monarchist pamphleteers.[27] No longer is it the deceitful language of the Church, the Court or the Sorbonne[28] which is in the dock: the accused is the 'language of the Revolutionaries', the language that misleads, the language that errs through malice or ignorance. Confronted with the aberrations of its enemies, the polemical dictionary sets itself the goal of rectifying meaning, of establishing it according to 'sure principles'. That is its mission, because a dictionary is 'meant to give a totally clear explanation of words'.[29] But that – as the 'aristocratic' author immediately explains –is also the ready-made justification for its own excesses: 'Forced to call things by their name, I felt that I had, in a Dictionary, to sacrifice politeness to truth'. . . By a convenient paradox, the requirement to be truthful stands caution for the 'aristocratic' author's own rhetorical violence; and the more the truth is blinding, the more the justiciary rage itself can be blind. The savage tone of the pamphlet no longer runs counter to the rules of the dictionary genre. It is an unavoidable consequence of it. 'I have sought to replace the epithets: knaves, blackguards, monsters, by others which are more decent', continues the anonymous author, {but] 'I have sought in vain'. It is from cruel, epistemological necessity that the dictionary becomes a tissue of insults. It is out of respect for synonymical accuracy that it is even reduced to silence. 'One article alone has remained blank: the strongest possible terms were just not strong enough to describe what I felt'. In these extreme cases, epistemology and professional conscience force the lexicographer into silence. Silence is the only possible attribute of the unspeakable. The article which left our lexicographer speechless was: MIRABEAU (followed only by the suspension points of an inexpressible loathing).

If, in the final analysis, the polemical dictionaries care little for methodology or scholarly guarantees, it is also because – over and above the normative effort that they have promised – they are making poste-haste, head-down, for that outer circle of the vocabulary which is no longer open to explanation or analysis. They can, of course, tactically speaking, arraign the words before the etymon, or before the tribunal of History. They always finish up, however, by pointing to that obscure zone (down on the horizon of a word whose meaning has been warped) where the language of the Revolutionaries – by its very abomination – is beyond any 'commentary'. Rational, regulated discussion of the new vocabulary must sooner or later be suspended for fear of indirectly legitimising it, because elucidation, even when critical, implicitly gives substance to the terms being elucidated. In refuting this 'inverse language' (as La Harpe will call it), our authors – by actually making contact with it – run the risk of admitting its legitimacy, and they do that simply because they have called it to account.

Such is ultimately the dilemma of the counter-revolutionary lexicographers: to speak about the language of the Revolution is already to speak it, to give it room and to give it houseroom. It is thus by an essential paradox that the political dictionary must suspend its own specific discourse, offer its silence as a superlative eloquence and 'be content with laughing out of pity'.[30] That silence and that laughter symbolically mark the *nec plus ultra* for a lexicographical enterprise which is faced with an agonizing choice: should it be edifying restoration or satirical demolition? should it be the authoritarian reassertion of common sense (of commonly accepted meanings) or a sarcastic paraphrase of the linguistic innovations? These are different tasks, contradictory tasks even, in that they suppose systems of writing which are not readily compatible. Each of the two mechanisms has its own dangers. If it confines itself to pastiche, the dictionary locks itself into revolutionary language: by dint of underlining its traits, it admits its force; if, on the other hand, it accuses revolutionary language of ideological impertinence, it confirms *de facto* its linguistic pertinence. Gallais, who is the most amusing and the most witty of all the royalist pamphleteers, opts completely for this type of irony. He plays – in the Sternian mode – at duping his reader; but it is also he (could it be in homage to the abortive ventures of Figaro in Seville?) who baptises his work *Extrait d'un dictionnaire inutile. . .* and who, rounding off in his 'epilogue', insistently reconsiders the futility of his work which he calls a 'pointless piece of buffoonery'.[31] If conversely, the lexicographer wholeheartedly takes on board the task of bringing revolutionary vocabulary to heel, the semantic order, which he restores, brutally and immediately brings in its wake a social order which is too low in repute to be acceptable, too discredited to be convincing. Calling a spade a spade becomes then quite 'impolitic' and can only – to use an expression used by Gumbrecht – convince 'those who think like you'.[32] The decision to be definitionally transparent, taken to its conclusion, indeed brings us face to face with the brutality of an order of discourse which is wholly identifiable with a discourse of order, and even with the discourse of one specific order – that of *privilege* – whose final word, the only watchword, would be: *status quo ante*.

If therefore (in their bulk and their virulence) the counter-revolutionary dictionaries dominate the logomachical arena from 1789 to 1792, their offensive is shackled from within. It is as if their mechanism is undermined internally. Imbued with a linguistic epistemology they have inherited from that Enlightenment which they profess to detest, they wear themselves out (and this is a crippling paradox) giving rationalist rectification to words when they are faced with a revolutionary language whose neological energy is less and less concerned with rigorous definitions. For caught up in the downward spiral of irreconcilable demands (demands that could be summed up in the four watchwords: standardisation, enrichment, rectification and regeneration),[33] 'revolutionised grammar' itself will soon be carried further and further away from its epistemological bases in the direction of that boundless sea, that sea of speech with powers of incantation, that sea of words with powers to compel. This is a momentum or a drift we find summed up by Mercier in one short line: 'Moreover, the word *liberty*, pronounced with feeling and conviction, has always been the making of a free people'.[34] By a strange reversal which is typical of the 'battle of the dictionaries', the counter-revolution of the years 1789–92 denounces the 'language of the Revolutionaries' according to critical categories which are those of the philosophical adversary, whereas (going in the opposite direction) the revolutionary replies, particularly from 1792 onwards, will not hesitate to invest the Word with an energy and a vigour which no longer bear any relation to a representative adequacy of the sign, even if that meant creating – in the words of their detractors – an 'inspired grammar'[35] or even a 'cabalistic grammar'.[36]

Seen within the dynamic context of this debate, or battle, the polemical counter-revolutionary dictionaries occupy then – on two counts – an important place in the debate over the language of the Revolution. Ultimately they prepare or prefigure the scholarly, articulate politico-grammatical counter-offensives. . . but not so much the 'providentialist' type we see with La Harpe as the resolutely rationalist type that we find with Morellet when, in Year IV, he sets about Domergue in his 'Leçons de grammaire'. But for the time being in particular, they force the 'patriots' to fight back on ground which, despite appearances, is not wholly favourable. For though, contrarily, the revolutionary camp says that it is capable of elaborating a coherent 'language programme', we will quickly see it stumble epistemologically (and often politically speaking) over the problem of language. And whereas our 'backward-looking' pamphleteers constantly rely on a type of Voltairian irony and an epistemology of the sign which is borrowed from the *Philosophes*, the patriots very quickly discover the inadequacy, in the revolutionary context, of that epistemology which is too rationalist, normative and static 'to be' in the words of Domergue 'equal to the Revolution'.

NOTES

1 D. A. F. Sade, *Notes littéraires*, in *Oeuvres complètes*, Paris, Cercle du Livre précieux, vol XV, p 28.

2 La Harpe's speech –*De la guerre declarée...* was published in Year VII, 1799, Paris, Agasse, p.18.

3 La Harpe, *Du Fanatisme dans la langue révolutionnaire*, Paris, Mignet, Year V, 1797, p.121.

4 La Harpe, *De la guerre declarée*, p.20.

5 La Harpe, *Du Fanatisme*, p.104.

6 Appendix to the *Dictionnaire de l'Académie Française*, 1798, p.vi.

7 *Ibid.*

8 La Harpe, *Du Fanatisme*, p.137.

9 *Ibid*, note, pp.13-14.

10 *Ibid*, note, p.70.

11 L.-S. Mercier, *Néologie ou Vocabulaire de Mots nouveaux, à renouveler, ou pris dans des acceptions nouvelles*, Paris, Moussard et Maradan, Year IX, 1801, p.xv.

12 *Ibid*, p.lxxiii.

13 L.-S. Mercier, *Le Nouveau Paris*, A Gênes, de l'imprimerie de la Gazette Nationale, An III Républicain [*sic*], vol I, p. 5.

14 *Ibid*, p.xxiii.

15 *Ibid*, p.xxv.

16 *Ibid*, vol III, p. 105.

17 Talleyrand, *Rapport sur l'Instruction publique* in the *Archives parlemen-*

taires (hereafter:*AP*), 1st series, vol XXX, p. 472.

18 Dom Jean-Pierre Gallais, *Extrait d'un dictionnaire inutile, composé par une société en commandite, et rédigé par un homme seul.* A 500 lieues de l'Assemblée Nationale, 1790, p. 191.

19 Adrien-Quentin Buée, *Nouveau dictionnaire pour servir à l'intelligence des termes mis en vogue par la Révolution*, dédié aux amis de la religion, du roi et du sens commun. A Paris, de l'imprimerie de Crapart, janvier 1792, p.20.

20 Abbé Grégoire, *Système de dénominations topographiques pour les places, rues, quais etc de toutes les communes de la République*, imprimé par ordre de la Convention [no date].

21 Quoted by Roger Barny, 'Les mots et les choses chez les hommes de la Révolution française' in *La Pensée*, no 202, novembre-décembre 1978.

22 Gregoire, *Système de dénominations*.

23 *Dictionnaire laconique, véridique et impartial, ou Etrennes aux démagogues sur la Révolution française, par un Citoyen inactif, ni enrôlé, ni soldé, mais ami de tout le monde pour de l'argent.* A Patriopolis, Aux dépens des démagogues ou Patriotes soi-disant libres. L'an troisième de la prétendue liberté; article REVOLUTION.

24 Letter from the King, in the Archives Nationales, dated: à Marly, ce 16 juin. Reproduced in *AP*, 1st series, vol VIII, p. 129. This passage was picked up by the press, cf *L'Esprit-des-Gazettes*, no 1 (July 1789).

25 25 February 1791. *AP*, vol XXIII, p. 519.

26 'Chercher une querelle d'Allemand' is a proverbial French expression meaning "to pick a quarrel with somebody over nothing" [Ed.].

27 Cf Ulrich Ricken,'Réflexions du 18e siècle sur l'abus des mots', *Actes du 2ème colloque de lexicologie politique* (15–20 septembre 1980), Paris, Klincksieck, 1982, vol I, pp. 58 ff.

28 The Sorbonne is here the Faculty of Theology of the University of Paris [Ed.].

29 *Nouveau dictionnaire français, à l'usage de toutes les municipalités, les milices nationales, et de tous les patriotes, composé par un aristocrate*... En France, d'une imprimerie aristocratique. . . 1790; Avertissement.

30 *Ibid*, p.3.

31 Gallais, *Extrait d'un dictionnaire inutile* , p. 78.

32 Gumbrecht, 'Persuader ceux qui pensent comme vous, les fonctions du discours épidictique sur la mort de Marat', *Poétique* 39.

33 For this aspect of the problem, consult my contribution: 'Le débat sur la "langue révolutionnaire"' in *La Carmagnole des Muses. L'homme de lettres et l'artiste dans la Révolution*, ed. J.-C. Bonnet and P.Roger, Paris, Armand Colin, 1988. This volume hereafter referred to as: *La Carmagnole*.

34 L.-S. Mercier, *Le Nouveau Paris*, p.xvi.

35 This criticism wa made by Morellet against Domergue in his 'Leçons de grammaire à un grammairien', *Le Magasin encyclopédique*, 9 nivôse An IV (30 November 1795), p. 9.

36 'I did not believe in the Cabala,' writes Buée, 'but since the Revolution, I am not sure what I should believe. Because what produced that Revolution? Was it not the different orderings of the syllables making up the words *aristocrate, liberté, égalité?*'. *Nouveau Dictionnaire*, p. 6.

ROUND TABLE DISCUSSION

In answer to the opening question (Jean-Pierre LACROIX): how many words in the French political vocabulary of 1789 were of English origin?, Philippe ROGER drew attention, not so much to the language as such, as to the sources of it: England and America. Recourse to English words (several hundred of them) was explicable by a certain anglomania (though on the decline in 1789) and, on the other hand, by strong Anglo-American sentiment. 'For example propagandists like Condorcet had been very active in the years leading up to 1787, widely publicising the American experience and, in particular, by publishing state constitutions, preambles to constitutions. Everyone – irrespective of political affiliations – had agreed, if for different reasons, that France at the end of the 1780s had no political vocabulary; the Revolutionaries claimed that it had always been forbidden and censured whereas even a Talleyrand said that the absolute monarchy had lulled it asleep. Importation of Anglo-Saxon terms and their rapid acclimatisation betrayed then a real need. The terminology of political organisation in 1789 is definitely taken from English. But a reaction does set in: linguistic awareness coupled with worsening political and diplomatic relations with England mean that, from early 1791, such importation (which is now seen as almost anti-patriotic) practically stops...though curiously the words already there are not censured.' Eric WALTER, taking up the latter comment, warned that 'the problems of anglomania and anglophobia are difficult to pin down because everything depends on the subject in question. Is it the English constitution, the English political regime or the English language? For example, Robespierre in 1794 suggests to the Jacobins that they should spend two months discoursing on the vices of the English government at the very moment when the people, the new Adam, had already very largely appropriated the political vocabulary currently in use which was itself English'.

Baldine SAINT-GIRONS, talking about the regenerated, virile language and vocabulary of the Revolution, drew attention in particular to the omni-presence at this period of the word *mâle* (virile) which she had often found within the context of the aesthetics, and particularly the architecture, of the eighteenth century. Since Mercier, for example, was well-versed in architectural theory, was it possible to see that sort of filiation? Philippe ROGER explained that the word had indeed been widely used, but also by people who knew nothing about architecture or painting (although, for Mercier, the hypothesis was plausible). 'As a word in use, it should perhaps be more clearly linked with visual representations of Hercules which, as Lynn Hunt has shown, had become popular when a virile figure was needed to incarnate *le peuple sans-culotte*. *Mâle* becomes a type of required stereotype in that "party-speak" which starts to take hold in 1791-92. There is an obsession with popular energy and that energy can only be *virile*. But it is by no means a one-sided preoccupation: Talleyrand, in his *Rapport sur l'Instruction publique*, talks about the "impoverishment" of the language in the past and explains it by an influx of flowery expressions; the French – he says – have adopted turns of phrase that are limp, that are more delicate than refined. His comparison (which is stereotyped) is between limpness/strength, delicacy/sturdiness. Note that in the eighteenth century the word *délicatesse* (delicacy) is quite pejorative. Conversely, the language – he says – 'has lost a host of *virile* expressions which it badly needs and which will have to be given back to it'.

David DENBY initiated a fairly substantial debate, via Mercier and La Harpe, on a closely-allied problem: the denunciation of the 'excesses of sensibility and sentimental language in the 1780s when sensibility was branded as (to say the least) excess and often seen, in fact, as a strategy for obscuring reality'. Philippe ROGER agreed that there was a link. 'Both La Harpe and Mercier were imbued with an epistemology, a tradition of literary analysis which owes much to Locke, that is to say a traditional critique of figures, or of linguistic excess, a critique of the language as something misleading. Two key things dominate the last generation of *Philosophes*: their very Lockian heritage leads them, on the one hand, to look closely at the abuse of words, the refusal to define and, on the other, since you use the word "obscuring", it also prompts them to criticise metaphors and images. For them, "obscuring" means abuse of images, the bad use of metaphors. Historically, this is the time when the distance between the terms of the comparison becomes such that the discourse, instead of being an art of illustration, moves towards being a technique for distracting the reader or the listener. That is a criticism essentially directed at Jesuit (and, later, Oratorian) education, precisely because their teaching praises the use of figures; in fact, the Catholic oratorical tradition is biased towards the figurative. There is a whole story waiting to be written about the position of the Jesuits and the Oratorians on rhetoric and the way in which they taught it'. David DENBY followed up by wondering to what extent it was possible to see links, continuities, even links of causality between the language and discourse of eighteenth-century sentimentality, revolutionary language and attitudes towards the language used by the Revolutionaries. 'I think that you have to define the corpus of sentimentalism in terms of narrative. I would use a model based on Propp's morphology of the short story: the narrative being as it were a place for negotiation between antagonistic forces and a progression by stages towards transparency and happiness. I think that you can see in the rhetoric of a Robespierre and a Saint-Just – who both have manichean visions – reflections of this discourse now starting to tip towards the melodramatic. There is an attempt to involve the listener (now rather than the reader) in the rhetorical procedures. And I think that somewhere in the sentimental there is also an ambiguous, and not always successful, aim to create an adequation between language and real life. There is, somewhere on the horizon, the notion that language can indeed express what has been experienced'. Philippe ROGER, though agreeing again, pointed to the sheer size of the problem and its multifarious perspectives (mentalities, intellectual and emotional ambiance, not to mention the generic problems): 'Sentimentalism comes to us through specific forms, which we have to define. Each single time we have to look closely at the filiations, at the interconnection between ambiance, mentality and genre. In a word, we have to conjoin the historical and the generic. What you say makes me think that there is a link between pre-revolutionary sentimentality and the Revolution. But if you stick to old- fashioned history of ideas, you can say both yes and no. Baudelaire, for example, will tell you that it was not the *sentimentaux* (the sentimentalists) who made the Revolution but the *voluptueux* (the voluptuous), whereas De Maistre – who has analysed tearful, sentimental discourse – says that the guillotiners were the *pleurards* (the weepers, the snivellers). But it is difficult to make progress with straightforward (literary) analysis. On the other hand, if you articulated an investigation into the intellectual ambiance with a reflexion on the evolution of genres, you would find something of interest, and I think that we could establish a clear link between sentimentalism and revolutionary discourse. I say this because you *can* find, in those very forms which characterise the period, this built-in articulation. Here I am thinking of the *récit de vie* (account of one's life) which lies at the confluence of a new form of self-portrait and the political necessities of self-description and self-defence [see Lise Andries, 'Récits de survie: les mémoires d'autodéfense pendant l'an II et l'an III', in *La Carmagnole*, pp.261-275]. This type of writing would be a good example of a sentimentality which reaches the sublime and which is the product both of cultural history and of predetermined political conditions.'

David DENBY also drew attention to another closely-allied phenomenon: the *fête révolutionnaire* (revolutionary festival), because the written text of the *fête* (which is its programme) seeks precisely to programme that adequation. But, on this occasion, curiously though unavoidably, the language – or what the language programmes – did not come *after* the experience. The language actually represents *beforehand* what the people were supposed to experience. Philippe ROGER – quoting Bonnet's work on Marat ['Les formes de célébration', in *La Mort de Marat*, collective publication, ed. Bonnet, Paris, Flammarion, 1986, pp.101–127] – saw the fêtes and their programmes as a difficult area because, as with the cult and celebration of Marat, we are dealing with a discourse which is an on-going allegory. In the case of Marat, there had been a master-plan to be used in each and every individual procession with instructions concerning the stations to be constructed (a court-room to symbolise his trial; the National Assembly to symbolise his status as a deputy; an underground refuge, etc, etc). 'How could you establish a link between that extreme and very stereotyped allegorisation and the *tyranny* of what is *experienced* (and which seems important in sentimentalism)? The intention of the parts is certainly to be seen as the adequation of language and experience. But the end-result of this collective phenomenon which was highly codified in political terms produces programmes which are ludicrous.' Peter FRANCE observed that sentimental language is supposedly founded on experience, but that it could become 'uncoupled' from it. When that happened, 'it can be criticised because sentimentalism is then the opposite of sentiment and experience. Think of Rousseau: with him the importance attached to the feelings can lead to a regenerated language. Or it can easily lead to silence, silence being the true expression of what has been experienced, that communion which does not need words. From that angle language can be extremely dangerous.' Philippe ROGER agreed that such a belief had been worryingly present under the Revolution. One had only to look, for example, at Saint-Just to see what he thought about language, laconism and the use of the word. 'In the political state that he envisages everything is done in temples. There is a passage in his *Institutions politiques* which is quite extraordinary, and it comes when Saint-Just quite coldly says: 'On n'ecrit point ce qui se passe dans les temples' (what is said and done in temples is not for minuting). What, on the other hand, saved a Mercier was the fact that he did not transport the demands of Rousseauism into his own political practice; he did not make the grave mistake of "totalising", of transporting the rousseauist 'exigence de la presence à soi et de l'expressivité absolue' into the entire sphere of politics. In my opinion that is what brought about Saint-Just's *Institutions politiques*.'

Joanna KITCHIN raised the question of La Harpe's appointment as a *professeur de littérature* to the Paris *Ecole normale* in Year III (1795). In her opinion it was curious, considering his attack on revolutionary language, that La Harpe the *reactionary* 'should have been called upon to teach the new rhetoric. The *Ecoles normales*, which had all been set up to renovate the broad intellectual sphere, were not particularly reactionary institutions'. Eric WALTER and Philippe ROGER believed that such a question could best be understood with reference to Thermidorian politics. The situation in 1795 had been complex and fluid, and – since the government did not have a clear idea of where it was going – it seems that it had operated a deliberate policy of 'ideological sprinkling', of appointing people with different political opinions. It had been banking on the fact that – given very great freedom of speech – they would spend their time arguing. Indeed the debates between the Institute, the *Ecole normale* and the French Academy (once resurrected) had been incessant. By not intervening, the Thermidorians appeared as people who censored no-one, who believed in free speech. Eric WALTER cautioned, however, that though there had been freedom of speech for the elite, this did not extend to the people or the popular societies. Any expression of collective opinion had been totally proscribed.

Nelly WILSON referred back to two essential features in Philippe Roger's paper which needed to be looked at more closely: to the idea of *regeneration* and to the closely allied notion that revolutionary language had been *cabalistic*. There seemed to be an interesting link here in the precise sense that the regeneration of the Jews themselves had been championed at that time by the Abbé Grégoire, who had had, on the other hand, an obvious interest in linguistic matters and the language of the Revolution. Philippe ROGER spent some time in reviewing Grégoire's position as a champion of Jewish rights in France (from his *Essai sur la régénération physique et morale des Juifs* of 1788 down to 1806) and in giving some consideration to the belief that, in order to be regenerated, the Jews had to liberate themselves from Jewish writing, the Jewish word, from the *Cabala*. When however the word *cabalistic* was used (and it was used on a vast scale) by counter-revolutionaries to denounce revolutionary language, it might appear that it was being used in the generally pejorative senses of: magic, occult or cliquish. And yet there are clear signs of a worrying link between the different senses of the word (even a conflation of those senses) which points to a strong undercurrent of anti-Semitism. Philippe ROGER revealed that, in a hitherto unknown and unpublished pamphlet dating from 1790, he had found the accusation that the Revolutionaries were wanting to replace the 300,000 aristocrats of France with an equivalent number of Jews who would be given citizenship [1790 saw Grégoire proposing citizenship for Jews as part of their regeneration]. It looked therefore as though it was against a background of political anti-Semitism that we should understand the upsurge of that word *cabalistic* which we find so often in counter-revolutionary analyses. 'Before looking at all these pamphlets, I had been unaware to what extent French anti-Semitism, which is well-understood within the context of the nineteenth century, is already being extensively articulated here in ways which – though not rationalised – were very elaborate rhetorically. I must admit that I was quite unaware of this. And the historians have not got much to say on the matter either.'

In the light of what had been said about the term *cabalistic* and the concepts that had been associated with it, Nelly WILSON wondered – since the language of the Revolutionaries had often substituted a new term for an old one – how the substitution of the word *Français* (the French) by *Gaulois* (the Gauls) had come about? Did it symbolise a return to source, a return to nature (cf. Rousseau and his ideas on language). It did not seem to betray the same anti-rationalism as the cabalistic terms. Philippe ROGER believed that, in having recourse to their mythical gaulish origins, the French were in fact having recourse to an *au-delà de la rationalité* (something on the other side of rationality). Because the rational position on language had been found insufficient, inoperative and little use to the revolutionary cause, they had had to find something else. Baldine SAINT-GIRONS pointed out that it could be helpful in this respect to look at the Comte de Caylus: in his *Recueil* [*d'antiquités*, 1752–67, 7 volumes] Caylus had given more and more prominence to the most ancient antiquities of France. In historiographical terms, the same *tabula rasa* movement had also been noticeable. People were tracing origins further and further back; they were going back beyond Greece towards Egypt, beyond Rome towards the Etruscans. And in the context of France we find Caylus going back towards Celtic antiquity. 'I do not know to what extent one can pick up traces of his influence, but at any rate there is a striking relationship between these different movements.' Philippe ROGER pointed also to the cultural popularity of the Celts (in the best-seller literature of the second half of the eighteenth century: Pelloutier, Chiniac, Court de Gebélin, Le Brigant). 'At this time too there was the on-going construction of a cultural myth about the Gauls which stood for the idea of a return to the purified (and quasi-inexistant) origins and which, on the other hand, was part of a historiographical polemic about the Franks (and the origins of the French monarchy and its legitimacy) which actually goes back to the sixteenth century. In the thirty years preceding the Revolution, the debate on the Franks once more becomes acute. To have recourse to the Gaulish origins of the people is then to adopt a political position, and this becomes spectacularly visible in our period with the famous text of Sieyès: *Qu'est-ce que le Tiers Etat?*'

Baldine SAINT-GIRONS suggested that while the dominant eighteenth-century epistemology was that of representation or reflection, it might be possible to find, in Rousseau, signs of an undermining of this epistemology which anticipated the revolutionary developments indicated by Philippe Roger. Philippe ROGER: 'It is evident that Rousseau's position on language cannot be assimilated just like that to what is happening in and around the *Encyclopédie.* I adopted the Encyclopaedists' position on the sign to show what it became during the Revolution; and the approach I found myself adopting therefore is that of the dictionaries and, in particular, of the *Dictionnaire encyclopédique*. What I wanted to examine was the way in which things changed epistemologically; but even the relationship between dictionaries is no longer the same because the distinction which the *Encyclopé*die seeks to establish between dictionaries of words etc is no longer pertinent in the case of the polemical counter-revolutionary dictionaries. They keep the original form essentially for its polemical potential and for the rigour of the divisions that it can make. What I set out to show was that it is this heritage from the *Encyclopédistes*, this heritage of representivity, this representation of the sign of transparency, this to-and-fro movement between the word and what it represents, which is the problem. If there is incessant movement back and forth between the word and what it represents without any obstacle between the two, then as soon as there is a new *thing*, you need a new *word* and, inversely, as soon as there is an attack on the word, there is an attack on the thing. That theory was adopted entirely by the counter-revolutionaries who set great store by defining words and who criticised the Revolutionaries themselves for not doing so. The idea of the transparency of the sign, which brings with it the requirement to be extremely attentive to the indignities which are done it, goes straight from the *Encyclopédistes* to the royalist pamphleteers. In the revolutionary camp, the situation is even more complex. In the beginning, they share the same epistemology as their adversaries with, in addition, a clear prejudicein favour of neology. But this prejudice is not particularly rousseauistic; it is in the tradition of the French Academy, which became favourable towards neology in the 1770s. It was, of course, the *philosophical* party (i.e. the *Encyclopédistes*) who controlled the Academy at that time. So, in the early stages of the Revolution, the Revolutionaries – if they have time to deal with problems of language and to reply to their detractors – subscribe to the "*Vulgate encyclopédiste*" regarding the transparency of the sign and believe, in addition, that neology is a good thing. On the other hand, their adversaries see neology as a bad thing because – as the inheritors of Vaugelas – they believe that only the learned may invent words (even then only sparingly). Conversely, they think that it is emphatically not 'on' to let everybody improvise linguistically. The Revolutionaries counter-attack only in 1792, and the whole thing then tips over into a dynamic which is essentially the dynamic of political combat, though the intellectual dynamic *is* there because they have realised (look at Guiraudet, for example) that they have no arguments against that adversary who corners them, saying:'First define, then we'll talk'. When they forged their politico-intellectual dynamic, they might have taken something from Rousseauism. The filiation is not clear to me, but it is something to be looked at.' Baldine SAINT-GIRONS said that what she found striking was the *poverty* of their neology; when one is looking, in philosophical terms, for the adequation of sign and thing, what is disturbing in revolutionary logic is that this adequation is not guaranteed by anything at all.

Bernard SWIFT (presently trying – as he said – to clarify Valery's attitude towards the Revolution) wanted to know whether the dictionaries of the period had analysed the possible senses of the word *peuple* in the context of the relationship words/ things? Eric Walter had 'spoken earlier of the *people: the new Adam* [see p. 18]. It seems to me that here we have the appearance of a new god. I say that because Valéry once wrote that "the word *people*, for example, had a precise meaning when *all* the citizens of a city could be gathered around a hillock, on a Champ de Mars. But the increase in numbers, the passage from the order of thousands to millions, has made this word a monstrous term whose meaning depends on the sentence in which it is to be found" [*Regards sur le monde actuel*, Gallimard, Pléiade, 1960, vol II. p. 919]. I would like to know what the Revolutionaries made of the word.' Philippe ROGER: 'In saying that, Valery is more rousseauistic than the Revolutionaries, even more so than Robespierre and Saint-Just put together! There is, in fact, almost always an entry headed *peuple* in the political, polemical dictionaries of the period which are essentially counter-revolutionary. On this subject, they tend overwhelmingly to give us a flood of insults, a torrent of abuse. But what I find interesting is that there is, in this respect, a cleavage which pre-dates the Revolution. It is one of the major problems and difficulties for the protagonists of the Revolution to make their *rousseauistic notion* of the people coincide with their *empirical images* of the people. Let us take Mercier, because he is both a Revolutionary and a Rousseauist (i.e. above suspicion). You find exactly the same cleavages with Mercier as you find with those left-wing pre-revolutionary right-thinking people like Holbach and Helvétius, in other words the cleavage *peuple/populace* (rabble). When he is talking about the language of the Terror, he says that its "expressions insignifiantes" (empty, meaningless expressions) had been capable of subjugating the French; but in that precise context he does not use the word *peuple*, but *populace*. . . and in another place the expression *classes populacières* (the rabble classes). So linguistically the problem has remained the same, whether we are dealing with the pre-revolutionary *Philosophes* or the revolutionary journalists and writers. When they use the word *peuple*, with an implicit or explicit capital letter, it denotes a sort of rousseauistic ideal collective (although not *necessarily* rousseauistic); but when they talk about the people *in action*, the problem becomes much more complicated. In general, when the people behave, they are the *peuple*; when they misbehave, they are the *populace*. There is, in fact, another way of approaching 'well-bred' reactions to this question, and it is through that marvellous incarnation of the people who appeared in the person of that deputy for Bourg-en-Bresse [at the Estates-General in 1789] whose surname really was *Populus*. He immediately became the favourite character with the most extreme royalist press. They invented a fable which lasted for two years, to the effect that Populus was the lover of Théroigne de Méricourt [the legendary Amazon of the Revolution whom the royalist press viciously slandered]. This monstrous couple – they claimed – brought forth vile, aborted foetuses every three months. We are dealing here, vis-à-vis the people in the period 1789-91, with an extremely revolting sort of royalist discourse, and above all a particularly vile discourse on women.'

Several people (Nelly WILSON, Peter FRANCE, Eric WALTER) pointed to the way in which the dichotomy *peuple/populace* was to be maintained throughout the nineteenth century, from Hugo down to Zola, but most strikingly perhaps in the case of Marx. The latter's version of the *populace* had been the *Pöbel*, the *Lumpenproletariat*. In fact, when Marx had created the latter, he had given a pseudo-conceptual existence to a figure which is the eternal figure of the *populace* (but now the really bad *populace*, the one which is the ally of the class enemies). Eric WALTER reminded everyone that there was another word, closely allied to *peuple* and *populace*, which had not been mentioned and which is to be found in Mercier's *Néologie* [vol, II. pp 380–1]; it was the word *prolétaire* which he defines, however, in a way redolent of compassion: 'Malheur! malheur à une nation divisée en deux classes nécessairement ennemies, celle des propriétaires et celle desProlétaires! Prolétaire! c'est le mot le plus repoussant de la langue; aussi tous les Dictionnaires l'ont-ils rejeté' (Woe! woe to the nation which is divided into two classes which are necessarily antagonistic, that of the owners and that of the proletarians! Proletarian! it is the most repellent word in the language; so all our dictionaries have rejected it.)

Three

DISCOURSES OF PATRIARCHALISM AND ANTI-PATRIARCHALISM IN THE FRENCH REVOLUTION

Lynn Hunt

The power of the French king was a paternal power; the king was the father of his people, and his authority as king was modelled on the authority of fathers in the family. Even after 1789, conservatives continued to defend the paternal metaphor. As one newspaper remarked in July 1790,

> Heirs of the *Franks*, who measured their own greatness against the even greater grandeur of their chiefs, let us fight, love, live and die like them, faithful to the principles of our Fathers...we were one great family assembled together under the eyes of its Head. . . Since we have all sworn to be brothers, we have a common father.[1]

Overthrowing kingship had consequences, among other things, for the paternal image of authority. When the French republicans abolished royalty, they not only had to find another structure of power, to write a new official constitution. They also had to establish another *image* of power, one no longer dependent on fathers in the same way. The answer, of course, was the famous French republican slogan, *Liberté, Egalité, Fraternité*. Universal brotherhood was the republican answer to paternal kingship, but it was to be a universal brotherhood – unlike the brothers cited in the above quote – which was not dependent any longer on the common father.

What I propose to do is to examine some of the consequences of that famous slogan and to show how ambiguous and difficult the notion of fraternity could be. In particular, I want to demonstrate that universal brotherhood left unresolved the position of women in the republic. I do not plan to tell you about official constitutions, laws, policies, political parties or individual politicians. Rather, I want to talk about the political imagination, the conscious and unconscious ways in which power is imagined.

In order to understand the workings of fraternity as a model for power, I propose that we think in terms of what Freud called 'the family romance'. When he used the term, Freud had in mind the thought patterns of a neurotic individual. The 'family romance' was the neurotic's fantasy of 'getting free from the parents of whom he now has a low opinion and replacing them by others, who, as a rule, are of higher social standing'.[2] When the child feels slighted by the parents, he (he, in particular, since Freud thought this tendency was much weaker in girls) retaliates by imagining that these are not in fact his real parents; his real parents are important landlords, aristocrats, even kings and queens. Obviously, this is not strictly applicable to the French situation since the political parents of the French were in fact already kings and queens. The revolutionaries were trying to imagine a political family that was not ruled by a king and queen. Thus I am using the term family romance to refer to the political, that is, collective unconscious rather than to the individual personality. By family romance I mean here more generally the development of collective unconscious fantasies about the familial order underlying revolutionary politics. The French did in a sense wish to get free from the political parents of whom they had developed a low opinion, but they did not imagine replacing them with others who were of a higher social standing. They imagined replacing them with a different kind of family, one in which the parents were effaced, and the children – the male children – were successfully, even aggressively autonomous.

Needless to say, the French revolutionaries did not stand at the tribune and lay out their psycho-sexual fantasies about the political order. They did talk about 'fraternity', the least well-understood of the values in the revolutionary triad of 'liberty, equality and fraternity', but in conscious discourse this was a political idea associated with equality, political solidarities, and the drawing of political and social boundaries within the community.[3] There are, however, all sorts of clues about the psycho-sexual meaning of fraternity in revolutionary symbolics – in, for instance, the ordering of festivals and the choice of icons and emblems – and, on occasion, in revolutionary discourse itself – in, for example, the debates on women's clubs or in the newspaper accounts of the killing of the king. The psycho-symbolics of the revolutionary political imagination are perhaps even more apparent, however, in a less conventional source: in political pornography. Here, however, I plan to confine myself to more conventional forms of evidence in order to show that even these can be read as revealing a family romance that organises important aspects of the political imagination.

The specific character of the French revolutionary family romance becomes more apparent if we explicitly contrast it with its American eighteenth-century counterpart. American revolutionary rhetoric was clearly preoccupied with familial analogies; in the most self-conscious way, the Americans portrayed themselves first as Sons of Liberty and later as Founding Fathers. These convenient labels are striking – especially in comparison with the French case – but they should not blind us to the complicated process of development that lay behind them. The notion of Founding Fathers was not invented all at once in the 1790s; it may not have been current until the twentieth century. But the use of the 'parent–child analogy' has been shown to be widely diffused in the political literature on both sides of the quarrel over American independence.[4] Peter Shaw, for instance, demonstrates the importance of children, both physically and symbolically, in the rituals of the American Revolution. In crowd actions during the 1760s and 1770s, Americans 'made themselves into children'.[5]

Yet by the time they came to write the constitution of 1787, they had developed a rather different image of themselves, or at least of their leader, George Washington. In the most comprehensive account to date on this issue, Jay Fliegelman argues that the Americans were revolting for filial autonomy from tyrannical patriarchal authority. They were not revolting against all notions of paternal authority, however, simply against the 'bad' despotic father. By mythologising Washington, who was described as the father of his country as early as 1778, Americans glorified the new, more understanding father of eighteenth-century educational tracts and set a moral example for themselves. As John Adams remarked, 'I glory in the character of a Washington because I know him to be only an exemplification of the American character'.[6] By the 1790s, then, American revolutionaries had transformed themselves collectively from political children into political fathers; the male leadership internalised for itself the role of beneficent father. The Americans were in a position, consequently, to imagine passing on their political patrimony through a contractual document. It may be that this psycho-political transformation outweighs in importance the specific details of disagreement between the various languages of American politics. Republicanism, Lockean liberalism, work-ethic Protestantism, and state-centered theories of power and sovereignty could all be accommodated by the new family romance of the understanding fathers, who ruled through wisdom rather than despotism.[7]

No one has undertaken a comparable study of French sources on paternal imagery. But, as far as I can determine, the French never called themselves either sons or fathers; they insisted instead on brotherhood. The notion of fraternity was not simply a pleasant icon for universal equality and liberty, a kind of good neighbourly feeling about one's fellow 'man'. It was rather a heavily-freighted psycho-symbolic story or fantasy (i.e., romance) that was critical to the fortunes of the Revolution itself.

I am going to outline in very schematic fashion the main stages in the development of the French revolutionary family romance, focusing for the most part on the images of fathers and children. But I will also try to indicate the ways in which this changing romance shaped the views of women in politics.

In the decades before 1789 in France, there were some telling indications that a crisis of paternal authority was brewing. Paintings at the official Salons were increasingly preoccupied with figures of old men who had trouble holding onto their powers. Rebellious sons were appearing with great frequency along with paintings that were devoted explicitly to Oedipus as an old and blind patriarch. The artist who went furthest towards imagining 'a new set of social relations' was Jacques-Louis David. Two of his greatest paintings from the 1780s, The *Oath of the Horatii* (shown at the Salon of 1785) and *Brutus* (shown at the Salon of 1789), offer new models of the family and of fraternal solidarity.[8]

These paintings cannot be read as straightforward translations of a new ideal of fraternity – in the *Oath*, the sons swear allegiance before the father, and in *Brutus*, the father has to sacrifice the sons to the well-being of the republic – but they do demonstrate a deep preoccupation with the relationship between family and state obligations and a striking concern with the links between masculinity and virtue.[9] These are profoundly homosocial works, in which men bond to the state through their affective relations to each other and develop their bonds in distinction to ordinary heterosocial family relationships. The gender differentiation of the *Oath* quite literally divides the canvas in two in a way that foreshadows the gender differentiation of republicanism.

In the painting (see Figure 1), the father receives the oaths of his sons to defend the honour of Rome, even against the family's own interests (for one son is married to a sister of the Curiatii, who will oppose him in battle, and the sister of the Horatii is engaged to another Curiatii – these are the two women in the foreground of the painting). David makes the sons the equal of the father; virtue is now passing from the father to the sons, and the relationship between the sons is as central as the relationship between father and sons. It is, moreover, the act of swearing fidelity that unites the brothers and that divides the men on the left side of the painting from the women on the right. Let me remind you, in passing, that the oath is a pure invention on David's part; it does not appear in any of the ancient histories of the event.

The gender division of the painting was not accidental, for analysis of the studies done for the definitive painting shows that David worked to accentuate the gap between the two sides. The figures in the two halves of the painting seem almost to touch each other in physical reality, but they

Figure 1

are as far apart psychically as possible. The world of the women and of the feminine is frankly devalued. On the left, we have verticality, bodily force, the resolute air of the brothers; on the right, passivity and weakness. The women, even more than the children, cannot stand to look at the scene of action. Moreover, they cannot speak. Words, the capacity of speaking, the right to take oaths as well as political action more generally are all on the left side.[10]

Parallel studies of pre-revolutionary literature have yet to be undertaken, as far as I know, but we might take the spectacular success of Bernardin de Saint Pierre's novel *Paul et Virginie* as indicative of a similar potential effacement of the father figure. Neither Paul nor Virginie have fathers in the novel, which gets its motive force precisely from the effort of families without fathers to confront the world outside the island paradise. Published in 1788, *Paul et Virginie* was to be the most reprinted of novels during the decade of revolution.[11]

During the Revolution itself, there were three main stages in the development of the family romance. (1) In the early years of the Revolution, between 1789 and 1791, the Revolutionaries thought of themselves as brothers trying to convince a good-hearted but obtuse father to agree to the reforms that they had proposed. We might say that at this stage the Revolution was driven by a generic plot of comedy, in which the sons seek reconciliation with the father. (2) The flight of the royal family to Varennes in June 1791 made a 'comic' ending impossible because it ended the possibility of a reconciliation with the father. The father had fled his duties and rejected his sons' efforts. Now the brothers saw themselves as embarked on a heroic quest to defeat the evil forces of counter-revolution on their own. During the period of radical republicanism, the brothers had to come to terms with the father once and for all, and the French tried to resolve the ambiguity of the political father's position by killing him.(3) Beginning sometime during the period of reaction against radicalism, but certainly no later than the Festival of the Supreme Being held in June 1794, republicans began to try to rehabilitate the figure of the father, and with it the possibility of reconciliation rather than a tragic ending. The Directory regime was, however, continually torn between different reactions to the paternal figure. Only with Napoleon would this underlying contest end; he would more or less successfully transform himself – or at least the ideological underpinnings of his regime – from a fraternal into a paternal representation of authority.

Not surprisingly, I see three stages in the development of the position of women that roughly parallel the three stages in the general family romance: (1) an initial period of confusion that was rich in possibilities and which included a surprisingly thoroughgoing set of new laws on the family and divorce as well as the beginnings of explicitly feminist discourse about the rights of women; (2) a period of crisis marked most significantly by the trial of the queen and the suppression of women's clubs in the autumn of 1793; and (3) a longer period of crystallisation and working through of attitudes about women, which gave birth to the distinctively modern forms of domestic ideology.

I want to emphasise from the beginning that these three stages include both conscious and unconscious elements. The problem of the role of women included on the one hand such self-conscious policy decisions as the granting of equal rights in divorce to women (by the law of 20 September 1792) and on the other hand issues with far-reaching unconscious resonance such as the preoccupation with sexual differentiation. The print entitled the 'Grand Débandement de l'Armée Anticonstitutionelle' (see Figure 2) shows quite convincingly that sexual issues were tied up with politics; it was run off sometime during the period 1790–91 as a counter- revolutionary statement, but it is filled with ambiguities: the army of the emperor can't 'keep it up' faced with the 'République' of Théroigne de Méricourt, a noted democrat, and with the 'Villettes' of leading aristocratic women who have gone over to the side of the patriots – the Villettes being a clear reference to the patriot aristocrat and supposedly homosexual marquis de Villette, who was regularly lam-

Figure 2

pooned in rightwing newspapers. This print calls out for a more extended analysis, which I won't go into here – just note, among other things, the sausages and hams hanging from the pikes of the sans-culottes and Jacobins, who hide behind the backsides of their women.

Let me turn now to a brief description of the three stages of the family romance. The first stage, which certainly begins before 1789 and perhaps as early as 1774, with Louis XVI's accession to the throne, is marked by the hope, and the hope deceived, of finding the good father. An engraving, 'Preparing the Champ de Mars', shows an example of the 'comic' father, that is, the father reconciled to his need for accommodation to the demands of the sons, who is now ready to join his family as an equal rather than as a patriarch. It is evident that I want to read an image such as this one as more than a representation of a specific event – the preparations for the Festival of Federation in 1790 – and more even than a sign of ongoing political struggles of the conscious sort – such as the effort to establish a constitutional monarchy. The engraved image includes a narrative as well as a representation, a narrative of the family romance, about what the French expected of a father-king.

This image of the reconciled father has to be juxtaposed, however, with a whole series of images that were devoted to denigrating the image of the royal family (see, for example, Figure 3 which is pornographic, showing

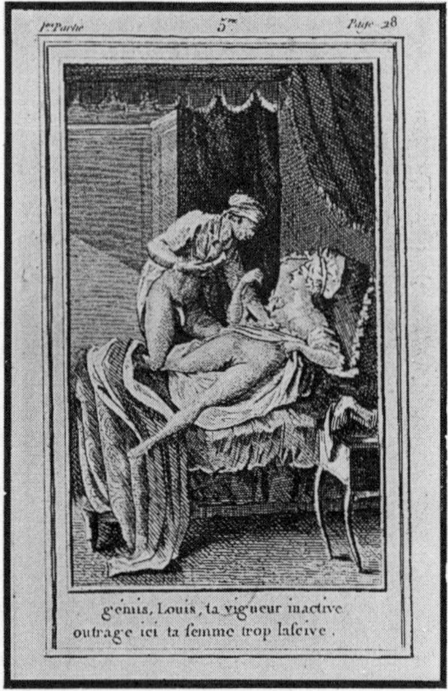

Figure 3

the king impotent). Here we see the hope deceived, the father being rejected. And, we might add, the mother not only being rejected but also being held in some way accountable for the failure of the father. In order to establish a new family romance based on fraternity, the old one of patriarchal kingship had to be destroyed. All possibility of reconciliation with the father was here denied, and the distance between father and sons was obliterated as the king became an animal, lower even than his human subjects, or a pathetic ordinary man incapable of establishing his own succession.

Central to this denigration of the political father was the parallel vilification of his wife, Marie-Antoinette. The queen was the subject of increasingly hostile attacks in the form of clandestine pornographic pamphlets that purported to describe in graphic detail her sexual debaucheries. The attacks on the queen began as early as 1774 and continued right up to and even beyond her execution in October 1793. The foremost expert on the subject found 126 pamphlets which he could classify in the genre of Marie-Antoinette, libertine.[12] Even before the notorious Diamond Necklace Affair of 1785 and continuing long after it, the queen was the focus of a growing literature of derision that was preoccupied with her sexual body. Chief among the charges against the queen were lesbianism and incest. She was accused of taking various of her ladies-in-waiting as lovers and frequently charged with having an affair with the king's own brother, the Comte d'Artois. These charges served to impugn her capacities as mother of the heir to the throne; many pamphlets claimed other leading aristocrats, such as the king's brother, as the real father of her children. Thus, attacks on the queen served to undermine the legitimacy of the royal line itself.

Figure 4, an anonymous print showing three soldiers, (one of my most precious discoveries in the Cabinet des Estampes) will serve as an emblem for the second stage in the family romance, the stage of 'pure' fraternity, from 1792 to 1794. It shows how David's theme of the oath was taken up in the period of republican radicalism. Here the brothers eagerly take up the challenge to go off and fight the forces of evil. The note of tragedy is already apparent; one brother lies dying, a portent of the fate awaiting the others. This is another oath between men who are perhaps brothers of the same family but who are in any case revolutionary brothers. The army has created its own family composed entirely of brothers. The three brothers swear their fidelity to the Republic in front of a man who himself is more fraternal than paternal (despite his reference to 'mes chers enfants'). The father is now absent, and the brothers unite to take his place. The feminine world is here in suspense, or at least, outside the world of action.

The representation of the new oath between brothers was made possible by the actual murder of the father, which structured in the most profound way the revolutionary understanding of fraternity. In January 1793, the Convention ordered the killing of the king, and the band of brothers took complete charge, after what some radical newspapers self-consciously described as a ritual sacrifice. The *Révolutions de Paris* editorialised in this way:

> We owe to the earth, since we have in a manner of speaking consecrated slavery by our example, we owe a great lesson in the person of the 66th king, more criminal than all his predecessors taken together. The blood of Louis Capet, shed by the blade of the law on 21 January 1793, cleanses us of a stigma of 1300 years. . . Liberty resembles that divinity of the Ancients which one cannot make auspicious and favourable except by offering to it in sacrifice the life of a great culprit.

The paper then described the scene at the scaffold, in which people ran up to dip their pikes and handkerchiefs in the blood of the king. One zealot sprinkled blood on the crowd and shouted, 'Brothers, they tell us that the blood of Louis Capet will fall again on our heads; well, so be it, let it fall... Republicans, the blood of a king brings happiness.'[13]

This is one of those rare occasions when revolutionary discourse is most self-revealing about the psycho-sexual foundations of the political order.

Figure 4

It is clear even from this brief passage that the revolutionaries themselves sensed that they were enacting or re-enacting a kind of primal scene, akin to 'that first great act of sacrifice' described by Freud in his controversial *Totem and Taboo.*[14] Except that in Freud's analysis, the brothers must always satisfy their 'longing for the father' by recreating him through gods and social organisation itself. But in contrast to the Americans, the French mythologised no living leader (at least not until Napoleon organised his own cult). They did not have a good father figure such as George Washington. Mirabeau, La Fayette, Marat, Danton and Robespierre all passed from the scene without establishing an enduring cult of their own persons. Moreover, none of them successfully represented themselves either collectively or individually as fathers of the country. Instead, they established a republic that was most enduringly symbolised by a female figure, Marianne, the goddess of Liberty.

Before you conclude that the republicans were true feminists, let me hasten to add that Marianne did not stand for female power. She was chosen as the symbol of the Republic because she did not represent any real person; she was an abstraction, a quality, and as such, above politics. The reactions to Marie-Antoinette showed how suspicious the Revolutionaries were of women's meddling in the public sphere. These views were shared by many women as well. In a tract on *Les Crimes des reines de France* (1791), the radical militant Louise de Keralio warned her readers that 'a woman who becomes queen changes sex'.[15]

Even more striking, however, was the denunciation of women who were active in political clubs. Just two weeks after the execution of the queen (which took place on 16 October 1793), the Convention discussed the participation of women in politics, in particular the women's club called the Club des Citoyennes républicaines révolutionnaires. The Jacobin deputy Fabre d'Eglantine insisted that 'these clubs are not composed of mothers of families, daughters of families, sisters occupied with their younger brothers or sisters, but rather of adventuresses, knight-errants, emancipated women, amazons'.[16] To re-establish the 'natural order' and prevent the 'emancipation' of women from their familial identity, the deputies solemnly outlawed all women's clubs.

Yet, though the deputies were negative about women's participation in the public sphere, they were at the same time unwilling to re-establish a paternalist vision of the Republic. Most representations of the Republic were feminine and they almost always showed young women, often virginal, but sometimes with very young children. But there is never a father present. In the iconography of the radical period of the French Revolution, there were virtually no emblems of fatherhood. The male representation of the people in the form of Hercules was shown as a virile brother (see Figure 5); we know that he is a brother because he is shown with his sisters, liberty and equality, who cannot be imagined as wives, much less mothers, if only because there are always two of them.[17] Indeed, one might argue that the incest taboo is not being very well enforced iconographically. This is a family without parentage, without a lineage. It is a family, consequently, that has trouble passing on its political patrimony (it has trouble constituting itself and hence trouble finding a suitable constitution). Is it too much to suggest that it is far from accidental that the two great radical spokesmen, Robespierre and St Just, were bachelors? Certainly, the authors of the Constitution of the Year III did not think so since they required all deputies in the Council of Ancients to be either married or widowed.

The third stage in the family romance, the search for a viable form of paternity, has been largely ignored in most studies of revolutionary iconography or rhetoric. The turning point in radical republicanism seems to have occurred in the period of time between the suppression of women's clubs and the Festival of the Supreme Being. A representation of this Festival, organised near the end of Robespierre's regime, shows the father present as part of the family, but he is hardly dominant. If the Supreme Being itself is supposed to be paternal and masculine, it is not obvious here. It may be that the gender ambiguity of the Supreme Being is itself a sign

Figure 5

of revolutionary uncertainty about the future of the paternal.

After the fall of Robespierre and the dismantling of the radical Republic, there was a kind of profound uneasiness about which direction to follow. The liberal republicans of the Directory regime had no intention of reviving monarchy and with it patriarchalism, but they wanted to distance themselves from what were widely perceived as the horrors of the Terror. In a sense, they were looking for the good father, a good father who was, however, only ordinary, only one of many fathers, a father who was not himself the object of worship.

The role of women was to be much more definitively circumscribed after 1794, but the principles for their exclusion from the public sphere had already been laid out in 1793. The deputy Amar, speaking for the Committee of General Security of the Convention, laid out the official rationale for a separation of women from the public sphere:

> The private functions for which women are destined by their nature are related to the general order of society; this social order results

> from the differences between man and woman. Each sex is called to the kind of occupation which is fitting for it. . . Man is strong, robust, born with great energy, audacity and courage. . . In general, women are ill suited for elevated thoughts and serious meditations, and if, among ancient peoples, their natural timidity and modesty did not allow them to appear outside their families, then in the French Republic do you want them to be seen coming into the gallery to political assemblies as men do?

When Amar asked the Convention whether 'women can exercise political rights', he answered 'no', but his *no* had a new basis in biology. Amar rested his case on both custom (*les moeurs*) and nature, but he emphasized the latter when he referred to the belief that 'women are disposed by their organization to an overexcitement (*une exaltation*) which would be fatal in public affairs'. In subsequent years, such thinking was developed further by French doctors and philosophers such as Jacques Louis Moreau (de la Sarthe), who published in 1803 his influential work on *L'Histoire naturelle de la femme*.

Fathers had been at least partially effaced, and women were now relegated to their supposedly "natural" place in the private sphere, but children were just coming into their own after 1794. The child took on a heroic aura beginning with Robespierre's last-gasp attempt to inaugurate a cult of Bara, the young republican martyr of the Vendée (see Figure 6). Bara was the model of the young hero with an innocent and pure body, but he was also a young boy without a father who, according to the many revolutionary engravings on the theme, supported his mother with his soldier's pay. Similar in thematic reference were the engravings of the young Darrudder, a drummer boy of fourteen, who, seeing his father die at his side, grabbed his pistol and shot at the enemy. Here again, the father is dead, and it is precisely the absence of the father that makes the courage of the son so moving.

The growing interest in children seemed to go hand in hand with an increased concern for the family as the bedrock of society. A comparison of exhibition lists for the salons of 1793 and 1799 shows a doubling in the proportion of paintings devoted to family scenes.[18] The 1793 salon saw hardly any paintings of fathers besides the one based on David's *Oath* by Petit-Coupray, which showed two young brothers taking an oath to their father to defend the fatherland. More fathers appeared in the paintings of 1799, but they were often fathers of fragile, even partially destroyed families. One prominent theme was Cincinnatus at his plough after having been abandoned by his son. Brutus appears at the moment of having to leave his wife Porcia; Marcus Sextus returns to find his daughter in tears at the deathbed of his wife. In many of these paintings, children represent

Figure 6

innocence, charity, and the ability to begin again. In an allegorical painting by Mouchet of the 9th of Thermidor, for instance, innocence is represented by a child, who sits on the knees of justice. In the corner, a little genie waters the ground to revive the buds that the passage of the Terror has dried out. The family will be the hope of the future, but first it has to cross through a difficult period of torment.

The prominence of children, then, did not necessarily mean that fathers were entirely rehabilitated; often the children are the real heroes, not the fathers. This is most apparent in the novels and plays of the late 1790s, when children became quite the fashion. As one contemporary novelist complained in 1799, 'Children are a great success this year, and my publisher wants me to write him one'.[19] Pigault-Lebrun laid out the commercially successful formula in his *L'Enfant du Carnaval*, which went into seventeen editions in the thirty years after its initial publication in 1796. Happy, as the protagonist comes to be known, is a virtual orphan, like almost all the hero-children of these novels.[20] Born of a cook's one-time sin with a local Capuchin friar, Happy is brought up first by an evil wetnurse and then works in the monastery kitchen until he escapes and throws himself upon the good graces of a visiting English lord. After a series of adventures that range from the burlesque to the gothic, Happy is saved from execution by the 9th of Thermidor. He ends up in London, rich and married to the daughter of the English lord.

What is most striking in the novels and plays of this period is the fact that the children, like Paul and Virginie before them, are almost always without fathers: they are illegitimate, foundlings, orphans or, like Happy, virtually so. The genre itself oscillated between the sentimental, gothic, burlesque, and even the pornographic (an *Enfants du plaisir* published in 1799, an *Enfant du mardi gras* published in 1802, and even an *Enfant du bordel* in 1800). It cannot be said that child psychology was very well developed in these novels and plays; instead, children were important as social experiments. Like Paul and Virginie they represented human nature in the laboratory outside of regular social relationships. They were, in short, a way of thinking about the problem of regenerating society, precisely the experiment which Rousseau had outlined in his *Emile*, which Sade would detail in a different register in his novels, an experiment which the French as adults had just lived. These were children in search of their identities, having to rely largely on themselves and not on their families, having often to traverse the perils of possible incest that are associated with unknown lineage, in short, representing a version of the formation of the social contract.

It is a rather long jump from children to constitutions, and I have had to pass over the links in my argument all too quickly. I hope that I have been able to suggest to you the importance of familial images to the imagination of power. I have not had time to develop the links between the family romance and the more traditional notions of political and social outcomes of the revolutionary process. I can only suggest here the following link: the family romance of fraternity enabled the French to imagine a complete rupture with their past. This rupture could not be imagined without literally some kind of image, in which to express it. By rejecting their political fathers, French republicans were able to imagine a wholly new future. They hesitated to identify themselves as political fathers in turn because they did not want to fix definitively the revolutionary process.

French republicans were the orphaned children having to make their way in the new world of modern politics without any help from tradition or convention. This image of the wholly new, unfolding in festivals, rituals and everyday political gestures, produced a revelation that was at once very radical and very volatile. Radical in its imagination of new unconscious structures of power; volatile in its difficulty of fixing them once and for all. The sacralisation of any document, such as a constitution, was made nearly impossible by the particular operation of the French family romance and, in the absence of a sacred text, it was enormously difficult to establish political parties that could compete over the text's meaning. In this sense, the family romance of fraternity worked against the establishment of a liberal, representative government. But, on the other side of the coin, the same romance had far-reaching effects on western political alternatives. The idea of a permanent revolution, a permanent suspension of patriarchal authority, a constant reopening of the terms of the social contract – these had their own powerful and continuing legacy in the modern world.

NOTES

1 As quoted in Lynn Hunt, *Politics, Culture, and Class in the French Revolution*, Berkeley, 1984, p. 29.

2 From 'Family Romances', in *The Standard Edition of the Complete Psychological Works of Sigmund Freud*, trans. James Strachey, London, 1959, vol.IX (1906–1908), pp. 238–9.

3 Marcel David, *Fraternité et la Révolution française, 1789–1799*, Paris, 1987.

4 The phrase 'parent-child analogy' comes from Edwin G. Burrows and Michael Wallace, 'The American Revolution: The Ideology and Psychology of National Liberation', *Perspectives in American History*, 6 (1972), pp. 167–306. Jay Fliegelman, *Prodigals and Pilgrims: The American Revolution against Patriarchal Authority, 1750–1800*, Cambridge, 1982.

5 Peter Shaw, *American Patriots and the Rituals of Revolution*, Cambridge, 1981, p. 195.

6 Quoted by Fliegelman, *Prodigals and Pilgrims*, p. 223. On Washington as father of his country, see p. 200.

7 Isaac Kramnick, 'The 'Great National Discussion' – The Discourse of Politics in 1787', *William and Mary Quarterly*, 45 (1988): pp. 3–32.

8 Carol Duncan, 'Fallen Fathers: Images of Authority in Pre- Revolutionary French Art', *Art History*, 4 (1981), pp. 186–202.

9 Thomas E. Crow notes that in the *Oath*, 'The body politic appears in the form of the sons, its chosen representatives; they stand on an equal footing with the father as his multiplied mirror image and receive from him, in a charged and ecstatic exchange, the instruments of power. Virtue is no longer in the exclusive keeping of the old, but passed on to the young in a moment of triumphant celebration'. *Painters and Public Life in Eighteenth-Century Paris*, New Haven, 1985, p. 213. See also the analysis in Joan B. Landes, *Women and the Public Sphere in the Age of the French Revolution*, Ithaca, 1988, pp. 152–8. In what follows, I have relied heavily on Crow and Landes.

10 Crow notes the way David relegates traditional composition (the women in the *Oath*) to the 'devalued realm of femininity'. *Painters and Public Life*, p. 236. The growing concern with establishing the basis for homosocial virtue may have been reflected as well in the general rise of neoclassicism with its concomitant retreat from depicting French national history. Also relevant in this context is Crow's insistence on the radical (and I might add, masculine) characteristics of David's

style: the defiance of convention, the asperities, dissonance, austerity, and awkwardness. *Painters and Public Life*, p. 235. See also Landes, *Women and the Public Sphere*, pp. 152–8. For an analysis which, contra mine, puts more emphasis on the figure of the father in the painting, see Albert Boime, *Art in the Age of Revolution, 1750–1800*, Chicago, 1987, p. 395.

11 This is my impression based on the lists given in Angus Martin, Vivienne G. Mylne, Richard Frautschi, *Bibliographie du genre romanesque français, 1751–1800*, London, 1977.

12 Hector Fleischman, *Marie-Antoinette libertine: Bibliographie critique et analytique des pamphlets politiques, galants, et obscènes contre la reine. Précédée de la réimpression intégrale de quatre libelles rarissimes et d'une histoire des pamphlétaires du règne de Louis XVI*, Paris, 1911.

13 *Révolutions de Paris*, No 185, 19–26 janvier 1793, 'Mort de Louis XVI, dernier roi de France'.

14 Sigmund Freud, *Totem and Taboo: Resemblances between the psychic Lives of Savages and Neurotics*, trans. A A Brill, New York, 1948. I have developed some of my arguments about the killing of the king in 'The Sacred and the French Revolution', in Jeffrey Alexander (ed.), *Durkheimian Sociology*, Cambridge, 1988, pp. 25–43. The emphasis on the 'primal scene' can also be found, though not in a very elaborated fashion, in Ronald Paulson, *Representations of Revolution (1789–1820)*, New Haven, 1983, see especially p. 26. 'It is here that we find the central and most important aspect of the self-representation inside Paris: a tension of the stereotypic and the unique, of the symbolic and the representational, which is to say the regressive, which urges a return to the primal scene which Père Duchesne and others (in England Burke) knew as the real heart of the matter, a scene more primal than republican Rome or Lycurgan Sparta'.

15 Louise de Keralio, *Les Crimes des reines de France*, p. vii. The full title of the edition I used was *Les Crimes des reines de France depuis le commencement de la monarchie jusqu'à la mort de Marie-Antoinette; avec les pièces justificatives de son procès*. Publié par L Prudhomme, avec cinq gravures. Nouvelle édition corrigée et augmentée. Paris: au Bureau des Révolutions de Paris, an II. The 'corrected and augmented' edition dated 'an II' simply added material on the trial and execution to an already long version of 1791.

16 Fabre d' Eglantine, in *Réimpression de l'Ancien Moniteur*, vol. 18, p. 290 (Session of 8 Brumaire, Year II, 29 October 1793).

17 See also figure 12 in Hunt, *Politics, Culture and Class*.

18 This is based on my review of Jules-Joseph Guiffrey (ed.), *Collection des livrets des anciennes expositions depuis 1673 jusqu'en 1800*, 43 vols, Paris, 1869–1872. I used the *livrets* for the salons of 1793 and 1799.

19 Patrizia Oppici, *Bambini d'inchiostro: Personaggi infantile et 'sensibilité' nella letteratura francese dell ultimo Settecento*, Pisa, 1986, p. 19. My account of the novels and plays of the Directorial period is taken from this useful little monograph.

20 I read the edition published in the *Oeuvres complètes*, Paris, Degorce-Cadot (no date).

ROUND TABLE DISCUSSION

Asked by Nelly WILSON to comment on the mother image presented by La France, Lynne HUNT agreed that – though she had examined in detail the engravings which were meant to be vignettes of power – it would indeed be worth while to excavate not only the imagery of mothers and fathers as it related to the evolving political situation, but also the whole trajectory of the representation of La France because it needed to be studied in its own right. From what she had seen, there was an ambiguity in the representation of this figure: sometimes it was maternal, at others not. The problem of *Marianne*, also raised by Nelly WILSON, was however somewhat better known: 'This problem has been worked on by Mona Ozouf, who argues that Marianne began, as many things did, as a *counter- revolutionary* naming. It was picked as a name because it was common; it was a name meant to be derisory, to denote contemptuously a *fille publique* (a whore), a *fille du peuple* (a female nobody). Then it was recuperated by the Revolutionaries and made into something affectionate. . . although we have to wait for the Third Republic before she represents an affectionate denomination of the symbol for the Republic. As for her being the subconscious representation of the Virgin Mary, this is something that Maurice Agulhon has written about at length [*Marianne au combat. L'imagerie et la symbolique républicaines de 1789 à 1880*, Flammarion, 1979]. Clearly we are dealing with an over-determination of the female figure because all the iconographical dictionaries call for the representation of *qualities* by *feminine figures*, and Catholicism gives pride of place to one central female figure. All these things do come together here, but with an important political dimension: it was essential to find a symbol not identified with the person of the King or of a living politician.' Neither Jennifer BIRKETT nor Eric WALTER were too sure about the 'femininity' of Marianne under the Revolution. 'The problem,' said Jennifer BIRKETT, 'is particularly knotty if we go on to speak of the new 'feminine' images of authority replacing the Father. Marianne has all the accessories of phallic power: rigidly upright in her long robes, carrying a spear, and what looks like a fasces. This woman in the Father gone undercover. To find a distinctively different feminine figure of power, you have to wait for someone like Delacroix's Liberty on the Barricades: a bare-breasted Maenad, pushing forward, with a whole collectivity thronging behind her.' Eric WALTER suggested that 'Marianne is less an allegory, with an exclusively feminine identity, than a bi-sexual androgynous figure in feminine form. It is at one and the same time *guerrière* (warlike) and *nourricière* (the nourisher). It is the *rassembleuse* (the rallier), the *Mère-Patrie*, the *Peuple-Nation* (that Michelet would have liked to call *la Matrie*). We only have to look – in the various representations – at the attributes (heaped) on her head: phrygian bonnet with its phallic bulge, or the cockerel perched on her helmet.'

Taking up a comment also made by Eric WALTER on Michelet's obsession with the gender of *Histoire* ('the term *Histoire* that we stupidly put in the feminine, is a rough and savage male' [*La Femme*, Flammarion, Champs, p 148]), Alain BOURDON and Bert HALSALL both expressed interest in *la* Patrie, not only in its allegorisation but also in the linguistic problems which it posed. What gender was it visually? Lynn HUNT: 'I have seen representations of *la Patrie* as a woman with many other figures in attendance. But what interests me here, looking at the problem from a different angle, is the increasing rarity of any imagery that shows united conventional families as units of the political order, either on the imaginary level of the Republic or even in terms of the representation of revolutionary events. You rarely see families acting together. (That has to do with the fact that there is supposd to be a separation between the family and the public sphere.) When I looked up all the engravings of the women's march to Versailles, there was only one that showed a child in it. But – to return to your question – I know of no male representation of *la Patrie*..' Bert HALSALL followed up this problem of *France, Patrie, Mère* (feminine nouns and usually abstractions of feminine figures, which pointed to the existence of a primary linguistic category that is found in any language with signs gendered towards substantives), by asking whether the absence of any paternal figure similar to Washington in French iconography might not also have a linguistic explanation. Lynn HUNT: 'What is so striking in the American case is the overwhelming need to make Washington into a father figure (even though he himself had no children); it is an attempt to create a revived, benevolent, paternal imagery which was military (but not too militarised, so as not to have connotations of warrior mentality). Washington is put in a symbolic position – and everyone is very aware of that position – the moment he is made Commander-in-Chief. He was truly created by the needs of the situation. In the war he is *not* a political figure, although in a sense he is elected a political figure because that is what is required to establish the Republic. This is very similar to the French who attempt to create an alternative imaginary system. This is what makes the interest of these allegorical issues, in other words: how do you imagine power if you give up, or overthrow, the old absolutist, paternalist, natural, traditional order? The interesting implications of this are: how is power thinkable? how can it be reconstructed? The American case is interesting because it is the one other place, apart from France, where there is a major attempt to elaborate an entirely new symbolics of power.'

Siân REYNOLDS asked Lynn HUNT for some elaboration on the women's clubs: 'The early ones were much like late eighteenth-century forms of male sociability and often had – as in Freemasons' Lodges – a philanthropic aim, though they were not philanthropic in the sense of poor-relief. They were ways of organising women's activities for the benefit of the Nation. Most of them were initially designed to gather jewelry and money for the sake of the government. Later, in 1793, comes the formation of much more explicitly political clubs, especially the Club des Citoyennes républicaines révolutionnaires which was by far the most radical, and which did discuss women's participation in the public sphere much more extensively. There were also a large number of provincial clubs which seem to have been more restricted to good works on behalf of the Nation than to explicit political discussion. People have been trying to study women's clubs in the Provinces but have had considerable difficulty in obtaining much concrete information. For example, newspapers tended not to be interested in covering such meetings. But, for Paris, I should perhaps refer you all to Dominique Godineau [*Citoyennes tricoteuses. Les femmes du peuple à Paris pendant la Révolution française*, Alinéa, 1988], whose excellent overview of what was happening in the capital is a companion piece to Soboul's great study of *Les Sans-culottes parisiens de l'an II*.' Siân REYNOLDS added that political activity on the part of women had been frowned upon by the authorities. In an intemperate outburst (1793), Fabre d'Eglantine, for example, had described the women who went to their own political clubs as *not* women occupied (as he doubtless thought they should have been) with their normal domestic duties, but as *filles émancipées*, or 'knights errant'. 'We are beginning to know something about the real women who were present in the public galleries at the Assembly and in the clubs from Dominique Godineau. It is she who tells us that it was the women of an age to have small children who were less well represented in these political activities than unmarried young women (under 25) or older women (over 50), many of the latter having sons at the front. However, this type of activity did not fit conveniently with the Jacobin ideology under construction in 1793, that is to say: women should be supporting the Revolution *at home* as a resolute but subordinate support system (like the Spartan mothers of Antiquity).' Peter FRANCE asked whether the quotation from Amar (pp. 36-37) was specifically referring to the activities of these women in the public galleries at the Assembly in 1793, when the galleries had been at their strongest and when women had been most visible, or whether he was talking about the clubs as such. Lynn HUNT: 'It was during the debate on the clubs. But obviously it takes in the general political positioning of the women's clubs in the critical period of the Fall of 1793. The first move in the suppression of the popular movement is the *suppression of the women's clubs*, supposedly because they are aligned with Jacques Roux and the *Enragés*. But what is obviously happening at this time is that there are different levels of analysis which are confused and confusing. We have family law, for example (which is quite different from the issue of the representation of the family as a political unit) and then the issue of concrete political struggles. There is a problem concerning the relationship between the two.'

Joanna KITCHIN, referring back to the representations of Napoleon, brought the two problems together under a new head: that of legislation and the *Code civil*. 'I take it that you would see the main thrust of the debates in 1800 and 1802 as strengthening what they called *la puissance paternelle*. You would see this, I presume, as being socially significant and politically symbolic?' Lynn HUNT: 'There would be a tremendously interesting paper to do on the beginnings of Napoleonic rule from this point of view, because it is clear that there is considerable ambiguity about what will be the nature of the Napoleonic system. On the one hand you have the *Code civil* which is much more patriarchal in its intent than most of the local codes of the Ancien Régime (i.e. there is a deliberate investment in the ideology and imagery of paternalism in this regime) and yet a curious ambiguity about the representation of Napoleon himself as a figure. Look, for example, at the seal of the Empire: even the Roman references are somewhat ambiguous because they are sometimes fraternal, sometimes paternal.' Joanna KITCHIN: 'The term *puissance paternelle* which was used constantly at this time goes back to the beginning of the Revolution, but then the term is indicative of radically different attitudes.' Lynn HUNT: 'At that time it is found in the context of the laws, especially of 1790–91–92, which were self-consciously conceived as an attack on paternal authority in the realm of family relationships. This is the time of the new laws on illegitimacy, on the role of the father, on family councils to handle family disputes. On divorce too which represented a *direct* attack on paternal power.' Jennifer BIRKETT: 'You talked a little earlier about the "conventional family". On the basis of what you have seen, could you tell us about the conventional or the traditional family?' Lynn HUNT: 'Initially, everything depends on social class. Godineau has interesting things to say on the family in the working classes. You can also look at the *Journal* of Ménétra, the *compagnon vitrier*, who was an artisan in Paris. He talks at great length about his family, about his attitudes towards women and towards his own children (his daughter, for example, gets divorced during the Revolution). One of the reasons why I have been studying the novels, plays and art of the late 1790s is to see whether there is a strong revival of a traditional family structure after 1795. But one of the interesting things that I have found is that the novels, and even the plays (which are often based on novels at this period), and especially the early melodramas, are obsessed with *orphan* children. I am far from having a convincing analysis for this phenomenon because I am just beginning to look at the problem.'

Jennifer BIRKETT: "You mentioned that the daughter of Ménétra got divorced. I think that, if we want to know more about women in the Revolution, it is to the divorce law that we must look rather than simply to the icons and the rhetoric. I think that the 'family romance' glosses over the real question, which is one of property rights. Women's crucial function in the Revolution is as channels for the redistribution of property. What matters are the discussions on marriage and divorce, in which the conflict is over the nature of the dowry and the shared property, and what happens to it when the couple breaks up. Does the wife get a share? does it go back to her father's family? does it stay with the husband? What happens to women depends on the strength of the political will to break up the large fortunes. It is the same dynamic which produces the debate over the rights of children in inheritance. Should there be equal shares for boys and girls, older and younger children, illegitimate children?' Lynn HUNT: 'Research into divorce during the Revolution is fraught with difficulties, given the nature of the documentation and its deficiencies. By this I mean that it is not easy to get *qualitative* evidence. For example, going by the records, you would think that all women were being beaten, the vast majority of the time. What would then have been a conventional family and have constituted normal family relationships is a difficult issue. If, for instance, you read Madame Roland, and what she thinks of M. Roland, you would have a very strange idea of conjugal relationships at the end of the Ancien Régime!'

Jennifer BIRKETT queried whether it was entirely accurate to talk about stages in the 'family romance' which excluded the father figure. Paternal authority may have gone underground at certain points during the Revolution, but it was never entirely absent from the theatre. John RENWICK said that he also would like to comment on the 'family romance' – not in order to disagree with the broad scenario – but to suggest, with further reference to the father figure, that the three periods which had been delineated for the 'romance' and the activities/mentalities associated with it might not be so neatly divisible, even less so sharply contrasted. He felt also that there was a further allied problem which it would be necessary to examine, namely the close link between paternity/ fraternity. 'Let us start with the father figure because it *is* the more complex of the two. My reading is that the father figure was in fact there throughout the period, not merely in the finite image of Louis XVI but also, and just as importantly, in *alternatives*. These alternatives are very much to the fore during the closing stages of Louis' paternal/patriarchal career (1789–92) and can perhaps be best termed "living admonitions" to the King himself. But these alternatives continue to enjoy an autonomous existence even after the King has disappeared and when – according to the 'family romance' – they too should have disappeared. (You talk, I think [p. 39], about a 'complete rupture' with the past). I am thinking in particular, as is Jennifer Birkett, about theatrical representations of political father figures. Those plays which spring to mind in this context are tragedies, and these tragedies are the products of three separate generations: Voltaire's *Brutus* (1730), Lemierre's *Guillaume Tell* (1766) and Chénier's *Caïus Gracchus* (1792), all of which enjoyed considerable success in the period 1790–1795. Voltaire's *Brutus* (which made the dramatic impact that it deserved to make only during the Revolution) is an apposite example. Sixty years before, in the first draft of his play, Voltaire had placed in the mouth of the character Valerius, in conversation with Brutus towards the very end of the play, an interesting statement. Valerius comes back from the Senate and says to Brutus: "Seigneur, tout le Sénat dans sa douleur sincère/Vient de l'état en vous reconnaître le père" (My lord, the whole Senate in its sincere grief/has just proclaimed you father of the state). That second line was, in fact, to disappear in the definitive version; but, notwithstanding, the message was to remain just as clear and was perhaps even clearer for being unstated. And to underscore the fact that the name Lucius Junius Brutus had – some sixty years later – become inseparable, in the European public consciousness/political mythology, from the epithet "Father of the State", that selfsame accolade is openly used by Alfieri in his *Bruto primo* (1788). The message of both is equally plain: the biological father, in ordering that his politically wayward son be put to death (though it is well within his power to rescue him) affirms – by this excruciatingly painful act of self-abnegation – a higher, all-embracing ideal of paternity: he becomes a genuine father figure. Returning to our initial problem, it is interesting to note that *Brutus* was a popular play during the period 1790–95, knowing numerous performances and no less than thirteen editions [one in 1790; three in 1791; three in 1792; four in 1793; one in 1794; one in 1795]. There are then those fathers who lay down the lives of their nearest and dearest, all the better (paradoxically) to be a father figure and then those who – like Caïus Gracchus of 1792 – achieve in turn the status of father figure by laying down their *own* lives for the people. It is also interesting to learn that Chénier's father-figure play of 1792 went into six editions [four in 1793; two in 1794]. What struck me in particular when you showed us the engraving of Napoleon was the fact that he is characterised as being *le soutien de la France* (the sustainer of France). You will find that, in Chénier's final telling scene, Caïus Gracchus himself is also deliberately qualified as *le soutien du peuple*. I read all this as meaning that we are still dealing with father figures; and I read this also as meaning that the father figure of the 'family romance' does not disappear with the execution of the King: he lives on, in the theatre, in one respect as a form of *compensation*. And it is interesting to note that the decree stipulating that *Brutus, Guillaume Tell* and *Caïus Gracchus* should be performed in Paris three times a week is a Republican decree [2 August 1793; renewed on 22 January 1794]. But there is surely, in parallel, another form of compensation. You have said, rightly, that the French mythologised no living leader because they did not have a good father figure like George Washington [p. 34]. You also said that, 'in the period 1792–94, there were virtually no emblems of fatherhood'[p. 35]. In all the conventional senses that is perfectly true. But if the course of History had been different, I wonder whether Robespierre and Marat would not both have attained the recognised status of father figures? Certainly during their lifetime as Conventionnels – and their fan mail attests to this – both were seen by large sections of the community as a new type of father (or protecting) figure. (Talmon [*The Origins of Totalitarian Democracy*] might have agreed with this interpretation).

Robespierre was overtaken by events before he could achieve durable, iconographic status. But there may be a case (since Marat was gloriously dead long enough for us to see what happened to *his* memory) for considering those Republicans like him, who had died for their faith, mostly as victims of assassination (and whose heroic example was eternalised either in print or paint) as being, in their martyrdom, on a curious par with father figures. But again, by way of *compensation* on the part of an *orphan* nation. Jennifer Birkett has already suggested that 'Marianne. . . is the Father gone undercover' [p. 42]. In the same way, are we dealing, when we see these theatrical and political figures, with *father* figures – to paraphrase Oscar Wilde – that "dared not speak their name"? However, I suppose that, if we take Marianne as the example, it must be conceded that within the context of Marat and Robespierre there are elements of ambiguity: are they paternal or fraternal?' John RENWICK also added that, were time available, it might be very useful to investigate in parallel Robespierre's own apparent search for martyrdom, along with the closely allied republican notion of *heroic suicide* (cf *Caïus Gracchus*).

Lynn HUNT responded to the effect that her argument, schematic though it was, had not been intended to convy that there had been, in the 'family romance', three rigidly distinct stages. 'My main view, which I think you have supported, is that there is a problem, an ambiguity and a tension about paternity; that there is a fundamental preoccupation with it. Clearly eighteenth-century France is driven by patriarchal imagery and thinking; so it is inconceivable that a Revolution could decide to repress this aspect completely. My argument is that the rhetorical structures of the French Revolution, and the operation of its rhetoric, were such that – different from what happened in America – looking for father figures here was much more questionable and problematic than there. Washington is a creation of the rhetorical structure of the American Revolution. It is not that the French happened to lack someone of similar qualities. The obvious candidate was La Fayette. But I am struck by the *inability* of La Fayette, despite a *conscious* campaign on his part, to get himself inserted into that role. My argument therefore is that the structure of rhetoric makes this kind of mythologisation of one particular figure impossible. My point is that there is a problem about the role of fathers. The French find themselves in a novel situation – as the Americans had – of trying to imagine what the *affective* basis of power is going to be without a monarchy, without the whole system of social and affective relationships that makes the Ancien Regime work, trying to see what shape the political imagination is going to take in Republican society. The person who saw this best was Burke, who pointed out that the minute you attack one element in this system, everything will fall apart. What I am trying to do is to develop a different view from Burke's but with the same problematic in mind. All I want to argue is that there is such a thing as an issue about the modelling of power, about the way power will be imagined when you break, partially or totally, with the system of power relationships that you have had before. I think that all the points you make are very interesting, but I do not see them as running against what I said. I simply want to argue that it is something worth thinking about as opposed to arguing that I have *the* absolute answer on what *the* one 'family romance' of the Revolution is.'

Philippe ROGER, coming back to the comments made by John Renwick, said that he agreed with Lynn Hunt when she said that she was unable to see a *father* figure in Marat [p. 34]. 'When you look at him, there are two things that you can see: there is the self-portrait that he wanted to project and then the myths of reference that he used. When I studied Marat as a figure, I concluded that what he was attempting to promote was the figure of heroic suicide and, more precisely, of devotion.' Eric WALTER, taking up this point, developed the idea that 'Marat, that 'monster', who had died by the hand of a 'woman', who was herself perceived as an androgynous force, was rather in the 'neuter' category, or to use an expression of Michelet: 'ultra-sex', i.e. neither masculine nor feminine, but desexualised by his very polarity as a being which was in the realm of the infra-human, or animality... *or* of the supra-human, the divine [on the 'sex' of Marat and Charlotte Corday, see *La Mort de Marat*, pp. 218–19, 221–2, 258–9, 264, 272–8, 321, 352]. And that is what Chateaubriand, in his own manner, meant when he said that Marat was 'raped by death'[*Mémoires d'Outre-tombe*, vol. IX, p. 3]. His legitimacy as a popular journalist does not come from a tutelary and founding role (i.e. the Father) but from a sacrificial sovereignty in which the gift of his own blood justifies the call for a dictatorship and a purge, justifies his terrorist discourse of denunciation and the return to an archaic form of power: the 'devotio' of the Roman military leader, the pact with the nether powers.'

Peter FRANCE: 'Can we return to the question of fraternity, which seems essential. In any investigation, we need to know more about the use of the word itself in 1789–94, and when precisely it was adopted as part of the revolutionary slogan. In particular, we need to know how much it was a gender marked word, only applicable to brothers, *men*. Could it not like "man" be used by women also to connote general human solidarity? How should we interpret Schiller's "Alle Menschen werden Brüder" (All men shall be brothers), or Burns's "It's coming yet for a'that,/that man to man the world o'er/Shall brithers be for a'that"? Do these really imply the exclusion of women?' John RENWICK followed on, suggesting that this was an opportune moment to go back to the second problem that he had indicated [the problem of the link between paternity/fraternity], which could also be closely linked with another problem: the swearing of oaths. 'If we were to look at the phenomenon of oath taking, we would see that it was massively there from the very beginning. Without detailing the important stages in the rapidly growing ethos of oath taking, we should nevertheless home in on 4 February 1790 which was the day on which Louis XVI went to the National Assembly to address the deputies. It was there that he "spontaneously" swore an oath to uphold the reforms which had been voted already, and also to uphold constitutional liberty. The effect on general sensibility was cataclysmic: within the weeks that followed there was a veritable explosion of imitations. Because the Assembly, heartily moved (and not to be outdone), had quickly returned the compliment by finding a formula for a civic oath, which was then solemnly sworn all over France in the following weeks (and then on every conceivable occasion afterwards). It was from that moment on that the civic oath becomes a national, and even a *fervently* national institution. The text of the oath, which is significant in psychological terms, was as follows: "I swear to be faithful to the nation, to the law and to the king, and to uphold with all my might the constitution decreed by the National Assembly and accepted by the King". Now whether that oath was sworn individually or (as more often happened) in mass meetings, the result was the same: the swearers of the oath were both sons (of the father figure to whom they pledged loyalty) and *brothers* (in communion of civic awareness).' John RENWICK went on to give examples of the way in which, in the period 1789–92, and 1790–1 in particular, an ethos of closely allied interactive paternity and fraternity had actually existed, with the latter self-evidently coming inexorably to the forefront as the traditional, and traditionally understood, father figure became suspect or a cause for concern. 'It is the increasing "absence" of that figure which becomes progressively a cause for regret, despair and disorientation. And I suspect that the anger of a Saint-Just demanding the King's head on those two memorable occasions could well be the anger of a son who has been deliberately and callously rejected. I noted that you said in passing [p. 35] that some attention should be given to the fact that both Saint-Just and Robespierre were bachelors. I think that it would be just as useful to remember, in the present context, that – in terms of family status – both were, long beforehand, *fatherless*. Betrayed again! That is why I am tempted to say, taking them as symptomatic, and generalising outwards to all the committed revolutionaries, that it was not *they* who took the initiative in rejecting their father figure, but vice-versa. Having been rejected by *him*, they – the victims – were forced back, more and more not just on substitute father figures (as I suggested earlier), but upon fraternity as a necessary, but only partial, substitute for that absent/unwilling/unworthy father.' Eric WALTER – also seeing this as a deep-seated problem – pointed out that one had to distinguish between the concrete absence of a political father and the solid, all-pervasive permanence of what Lacan calls 'le Nom-du-Père' which, broadly speaking, is the Law. On the other hand, there is an obsession with the absence or the weakness of the father/father figure which haunts the French novel in the eighteenth century (Prévost, Rétif etc). The same obsession is to be found in the pedagogical novel, from *Télémaque* down to *Emile*, where the paternal function is taken over by the Pédagogue–Governor–Legislator: 'The latter is a very strong symbolical figure who was to be so dazzlingly promoted during the Revolution. I would also add that, from Rousseau on, autobiographical discourse accords considerable space to this theme of the absent, inadequate, irresponsible father. With notable variations, that figure is to be found in the novels and autobiographies of the Romantic period (Stendhal, *Henry Brûlard*; Musset, *Confession d'un enfant du siècle* etc.) down to Sartre's *Les Mots*: "Je n'ai pas eu de père, je n'ai pas de Sur-Moi" (I did not have a father, I have no Super-Me). There is an enormous amount to be said on the political unconscious among the French, *à propos* the politico-symbolic fathers that they have found for themselves, from Napoleon down to Pétain or De Gaulle. The problem is the same as the one raised by Lynn Hunt, but it would take us way beyond the bounds set for this colloquium'.

Four

SPEAKERS AND AUDIENCE: THE FIRST DAYS OF THE CONVENTION

Peter France

My aim in this paper is to characterise ways of speaking in a Revolutionary assembly.[1] I shall not therefore be concerned with revolutionary language in general, nor with writing and journalism (which bear a close and interesting relation to speech in many cases). Nor for the most part shall I be considering the theoretical positions on rhetoric and eloquence which can be found in various writings – and indeed speeches – of the revolutionary period.[2] Even with these exclusions, my subject is an impossibly large one, and I shall further limit it by confining myself to the parliamentary assemblies, saying nothing for instance of the way in which people spoke in the clubs, the *fêtes*, the theatre, the streets.

Over the last two centuries, this eloquence has been by turns neglected, vilified and praised to the skies, depending on the *parti-pris* of the writer. Against the violent abuse of a Taine (whose *Origines de la France contemporaine* continues a tradition of denigration which had begun even before La Harpes's *Du fanatisme dans la langue revolutionnaire*), we may set the enthusiasm of a Michelet, an Aulard or indeed a Roger Garaudy.[3] Generally speaking, in the manner of conventional literary history, the object of attention has been the individual author (in this case the orator). The two monumental volumes of Aulard, for instance, consist mainly of characterisations of the eloquence of particular speakers, Mirabeau, Danton, Vergniaud, Robespierre and many other less familiar names. In publishing terms, for obvious reasons, the eloquence of the Revolution has usually been represented by collections of major speeches, taken out of context. It seems to me, however, just as interesting to try to form a picture of how this eloquence worked in context. For this reason, in an earlier article, I studied in some detail the unfolding of the events of one particular day at the Convention Nationale.[4] Here, taking a rather different approach, I extend my brief to cover a period of five days, the first five days in the existence of the Convention, from 21 September to 25 September 1792.

The problem of sources for the study of speech is a difficult one.[5] In the case of the French Revolution, once one goes beyond the major speeches, many of which were published separately from the author's manuscripts and have in some cases been properly edited in recent times,[6] one is essentially dealing with records of debates either in the *procès-verbaux* (minutes) of the assemblies or in the newspapers. None is entirely satisfactory. The *Archives Parlementaires*, compiled at the end of the last century, bring together material from several sources. But these sources (and therefore their reliability) for the period covered in this paper are not generally identified. The *Moniteur* on the other hand is usually reckoned to be the best of the newspaper accounts, though it is often incomplete (stenographic techniques were rudimentary) and may be biased (towards the Gironde in September 1792). Notwithstanding their defects I shall rely principally on these two sources.[7] It has to be said, however, that even if one had a verbatim account of all that was said, one would still be far removed from the reality of the thing. *Actio* (gesture, voice etc.), for Demosthenes the be-all and end-all of eloquence, can only be guessed at, though sometimes with the help of contemporary accounts. Likewise the atmosphere of the assembly, even in the quite liberal sense of the term, was obviously crucial in these debates. The records give sparse 'stage directions' such as 'double salve d'applaudissements' (two bursts of applause), 'murmures' (murmurings) or 'Plusieurs députés s'élancent à la tribune' (several deputies rush to the rostrum), and these can be supplemented with pictures or eye-witness accounts such as those of Chateaubriand. This last example will serve to remind us that eye-witness accounts are only as reliable as the eye-witness. The present-day scholar is bound therefore to feel rather as the Russian critic Kazansky did when analysing Lenin's oratory: 'The text of the speech confronts him like a text written in a barely comprehensible language.'[8]

Contemporaries were conscious that the development of political oratory –like that of political journalism –was a remarkable new development of the revolutionary years. Mercier wrote: 'just as a prodigious change has come about in current circumstances, our eloquence has asssumed a new form.' [9] It had been a commonplace in the preceding 150 years to deplore the decline of political eloquence, which could not flourish in an absolute monarchy. The sudden explosive expansion of the political scene confronted speakers with the need to work out new forms of speech for the new – often disturbingly new – situation. There were, of course, precedents. Not a few deputies had cut their teeth in the law-courts, pulpits and academies of the Ancien Régime, and models could also be sought in the eloquent discourses of the eighteenth-century *Philosophes*, in the written records of ancient Greece or Rome and in the actual experience of parliamentary proceedings in England and America. Nevertheless the rapid and often violent development of events both inside and outside the national assemblies threw down a formidable challenge to the deputies, who could feel, without too much exaggeration, that not only their own fate, but the fate of the nation (or indeed of the whole world) hung on the way they spoke.[10]

Of the five principal parts of rhetoric, two (*memoria* and *actio*) cannot be used for the analysis of speech that has long fallen silent. Of the other three, *dispositio* only really concerns the shape given to set speeches of some length, and *elocutio*, while clearly essential, is of dubious usefulness when one is not certain of the precise words spoken. I shall not therefore be aiming at a stylistic analysis, but shall use rather two concepts belonging to the domain of *inventio*, which concerns the material of persuasion. These are *ethos*, whereby the speaker contrives to present himself in such a way as to win trust and carry conviction, and *pathos*, which involves the appeal to the passions of the audience. The third member of the triad, *logos*, or the forms and figures of proof, I shall omit for the present, since it is more complex and variable, less amenable to generalisation. I want, however, to begin with a category belonging rather to poetics than to rhetoric, *decorum*, since it seems to me that one of the crucial problems facing the assembly and its speakers was the elaboration of a code of propriety suitable to the revolutionary situation.

Before coming to this, let me say a few words about the moment and the place. There is no need to go into any detail about the political situation on 21 September 1792. We are in the immediate aftermath of the popular, Parisian insurrection of 10 August and the September massacres. This was a period of national danger, which was halted, for the time being, by the French victories culminating in Valmy (20 September). Danton is very much the man of the moment. The Convention, rapidly elected by a much broader suffrage than the previous assemblies (though with lower participation), assembles in Paris on 21 September, some of the new deputies arriving late. Hostile observers may describe it as being 'collected principally from the dregs of France',[11] but in fact its members are neither plebeian nor inexperienced in politics – if two thirds are new to the national assembly, almost all have been involved in regional and local administration.

A great deal of business awaits the new *Conventionnels*. They formally abolish the monarchy on day 1, proclaiming the Republic almost as an afterthought. Thereafter they are concerned equally to deal with current disorder (assuring some continuity in law enforcement, taxation and so on, and overseeing the national war effort), and to plan the future, which means above all working out a new constitution to be submitted (or such is the theory) to the people. In fact, however, the essential business is the coming to terms with the new developments of August and September. For the Girondins this means dealing with the threat to law and order, security and property which they see in the actions of the Paris Commune, and heading off the danger of a revolutionary dictatorship (that of Robespierre). For the Montagne, the threat is rather the Girondin conspiracy to defraud the people of their revolution. From the outset, in fact, there is a battle for power between the two groups (even if the demarcation between them is uncertain). The Girondins appear to be in control, their majority giving them key positions such as that of President of the assembly, but the Montagnard minority can appeal to their popular Parisian support, which is physically present in the *tribunes* or public galleries.

Besides having a clear idea of the political situation, it is also important to have a clear idea of the actual physical setting when considering these debates. Until May 1793 the Convention will continue to sit, like the Législative, in the Salle du Manège of the Tuileries. This was a totally unsuitable hall. It was a very elongated rectangle, with the President sitting in the middle of one of the long sides and the speaker's *tribune*, together with the *barre* to which endless deputations were admitted, exactly opposite him. The deputies sat to the left and right of the speaker, many of them far to one side, so that they could not hear or see, and were naturally more inclined to talk among themselves or interrupt the speaker. Along one side of the rectangle, but also at its far ends (in the latter case above the level of the deputies) were the popular galleries, which were to prove such an uncontrollable and powerful element in the debates. The poor audibility, visibility and ventilation had a considerable impact on the conduct of debates, as many contemporary statements indicate in graphic terms. Here for instance is Quatremère de Quincy, speaking to the Législative in October 1791: 'the present form of the chamber has many other drawbacks; it is very muffled.. people do not speak, they shout; the man who shouts is under strain and for that very reason he is ready to become violent; he communicates his state of mind to those who are listening to him.' [12]

Decorum

It may be helpful at the outset to remind ourselves of Grégoire's famous statement, made to the Convention on 20 Prairial An II (8 June 1794): 'Under depotism, language bore the marks of baseness; it was the jargon of those who were called people of good form (*gens de bon ton*), and who where almost always a disgrace to good morals and the scum of humanity. The language of Republicans must stand out by frankness, and with a dignity that is mid- way between abjectness and roughness.' [13] These words were obviously spoken many months after the opening of the Convention, and of course Grégoire was not mainly concerned with the language to be used in the National Assembly. Even so, he does give an idea of the standard Jacobin line on modes of address. Manly and noble simplicity, including *tutoiement*, is welcomed, but contrary to the views of a Hébert, vulgarity is rejected as unworthy of the new Republic.[14]

Now one of the stock images of the revolutionary assemblies, as of many other aspects of revolutionary culture, is of a world in which the old norms of decorum no longer hold and in which vulgarity runs riot. It is therefore worth noting that one of the features of the first debates of the Convention is the concern to maintain dignity and orderly procedures, to keep the tone of debate at a proper level. This had, of course, been a problem from 1789 onwards, and the successive assemblies had worked hard at it. One of the first motions on 21 September 1792 comes from the deputy Manuel, who speaks as follows: 'One must see here an assembly of philosophers engaged in working towards the happiness of the world. Here everything must exude a character of dignity and grandeur which will impress the whole universe. I demand that the President of France should be lodged in the national Palace of the Tuileries, that the attributes of law and force should always be by his side and that each time he opens the day's business all citizens present should rise'... (*AP*,69) The use of the word 'universe' takes one back to classical tragedy, where Racine's Titus had felt himself to be acting in a 'plus noble théâtre'.

Quite apart from the unfortunate reference to a 'President of France', Manuel's proposal is greeted with hostility. Gravely underestimating the importance of the symbolic, Matthieu ridicules the proposal, noting that 'Our predecessors lost much time in deciding what should be the size of the armchair for the former King'. More to the point, Chabot asserts: 'you can seek no dignity other than that of being one with the Sans-Culottes who make up the majority of the nation' (*AP*, 70). True dignity is to be sought in simplicity. Manuel's motion is set aside then, but the assembly returns constantly to the question of dignity. The first session has opened with a very formal speech by François de Neufchâteau on behalf of the

Legislative Assembly and an equally solemn reply by Pétion, the President, who proclaims: 'We shall engage upon this august mission with the deep sense of reverence that it inspires' (*AP*, 68).

What does this mean in practice? In the first place a certain formality of address. The Conventionnels call one another 'representants du peuple souverain', 'législateurs', 'citoyens' and so forth – and still, occasionally, 'Monsieur', though this is on its way out. *Tutoiement* is very rare. In the second place, a vocabulary that belongs to the noble register, free of all trivial and vulgar words. And thirdly, a high seriousness – there are, to judge from the records, few jokes at the Convention Nationale. An interesting exception proves the rule – and it is worth noting that here again it is a question of symbolism, that essential but vulnerable part of the new revolutionary culture. Immediately after the adoption of the new seal for the revolutionary archives (the birth of Marianne), there are proposals to eliminate the white from the *tricolore* and to do away with the *fleur de lys*. An unnamed member, no doubt wanting to get on with 'real business', shouts: 'I demand that these proposals be referred to a committee of milliners', upon which 'The President expostulates against this witticism as fitting ill with the dignity of the representatives of the people' (*AP*, 81). The motions are set aside none the less.

Laughter is a powerful, but unseemly weapon. Another threat to decorum comes from interruptions. From the beginning of the first session members are protesting at these, and insisting that all speakers should obtain the permission of the President. (It is no doubt significant that, from early on, the Constituante had decided not to follow the British example of requiring members to address their remarks to the President.) Naturally enough, interruption persists, though of course it is hard to tell from the written accounts just how frequent and rude it was. At one point on 25 September we read: 'A large number of deputies rush to the rostrum, all wanting to speak at the same time' (*AP*, 130) – but this disorder is apparently far from reaching the heights of the following April – or indeed of the recent events of 10 August.

It is noticeable that the speakers most often interrupted are Robespierre and Marat – in other words, most interruptions come from the benches of the Gironde. Accused of aiming at dictatorship, Robespierre launches into a long self-justification which visibly riles his opponents. At one point the debate reads like this:

> (*Nouveaux murmures*)
> *Robespierre*: Quand l'Assemblée ne voudra plus m'entendre, elle me fera connaitre sa volonté [through the President presumably]. Je sens qu'il est fâcheux pour moi d'être toujours interrompu.
> *Plusieurs membres*: Abrégez.

Robespierre: Je n'abrégerai point. Eh bien, je m'en vais vous forcer à m'écouter. . .[15]

The other main source of interruptions is, of course, the public galleries, whose noisy behaviour dogged all the assemblies until Thermidor, when they were suppressed. By the time of the Convention the social composition of the *tribunes* had changed considerably, with women of the people playing an increasingly important role. They usually favour the Montagne and, on 25 September, when they are clearly giving vociferous support to Marat against a hostile assembly, a Girondin member makes the often repeated appeal: 'I demand that the President call the public galleries to order; they are daring to mutter. They have tyrannized the Assembly for too long' (*AP*, 139). To no avail.

Orderly procedure was disrupted by interruptions, but the greatest threat to decorum was probably the use of '*personnalités*', in other words personal abuse. This surfaces regularly – and no doubt the *Moniteur* only tells a part of the story. One example occurs on 22 September, when Danton is arguing for having judges elected by popular vote. Addressing Danton, the deputy Chasset says:

> Avec ces flagorneries continuelles envers le peuple, on remettrait son sort à l'arbitraire d'un homme qui aurait usurpé sa confiance; ce sont des flagorneries, je le répète.
>
> *Danton:* Vous ne flagorniez pas le peuple lors de la révision.
>
> (*Murmures prolongés)*
>
> *Masuyer*: Je demande que M. Danton soit rappelé à l'ordre, et à ce qu'il doit à lui-même, à la majesté du peuple, et à la Convention nationale.
>
> *Le Président*: Je conçois que l'Assemblée, pénétrée de la dignité qui doit présider à ses déliberations, voie avec douleur qu'on les avilit par des débats scandaleux. Faisons-nous une loi impérieuse de ne jamais nous permettre aucune personnalité (*AP*, 85).[16]

The word *flagornerie* (toadying) does not seem particularly scandalous, and there are no recorded examples in these five days of recognisably vulgar abuse. It is not really surprising then that one person's abuse was another person's plain speaking. An interesting episode, again involving Danton, occurs on the following day. Billaud-Varenne has been causing a storm by accusing a fellow deputy of being a partisan of La Fayette – 'several members shout out the word *slander* : turmoil is to be seen'. But Danton defends such forthrightness with a reference to one of the great heroes of the age: 'In the Roman Senate, Brutus uttered truths which we, with our fainthearted standards, would call personal abuse' (*AP*, 112). Such brutual frankness is demanded of the honest republican.

Decorum collapses most notably in relation to Marat, who is the target of exceptionally violent abuse from many members. When he gets up to give what appears to be his 'maiden speech' at the Assembly, he comments on his unpopularity: 'I have then, in this Assembly, a large number of personal enemies' and the reporter notes: 'All! All of us, shout the whole Assembly indignantly rising to their feet' (*AP*, 138). He is referred to crudely as 'the most villainous of men and the maddest' or simply 'that man'. He is directly addressed by other deputies (this is relatively unusual), and what is more, they call him *tu*. This is not a sign of manly frankness, as in Grégoire's ideal, it is simply abuse. Apart from Marat, *tutoiement* is only recorded as being used for Robespierre during these five days. And whereas he replies with aggrieved dignity, Marat, who is quite capable of a calm and reasonable posture, does himself flout parliamentary decorum quite deliberately. A famous – and, it must be said, unusual – example occurs on 25 September. Marat has been speaking in favour of a temporary dictatorship on the Roman model. Greeted by jeers, he declares dramatically: 'I fear nothing under the sun, and I must declare that if I had been indicted, I would thereupon have blown my brains out at the foot of this rostrum' –whereupon he pulls out a pistol and puts it to his forehead (*AP*, 142). Not surprisingly, such a flagrant breach of decorum scandalizes. It should be remembered, however, that the ancient rhetorical tradition (as well as Rousseau's *Emile*) spoke of an eloquence of things or of deeds which spoke louder than mere words, associated often with a decadent civilisation. It is two new members of the Assembly, Danton and Marat, who appear most willing to challenge decorum in the name of democracy or republicanism.

It must be said that it is not easy to gauge the extent to which dignity is actually undermined in the proceedings of the Convention Nationale on these days. What are we to understand by 'murmures'? A gentle ripple or a violent storm? Nor should one, by way of comparison, have too exalted an idea of the decorum of such a model as an English House of Commons, where interruption and general noise were endemic. [17] Even so, the overall impression created by a study of these days – and others like them – is of an attempt, in some quarters at least, to hang on to a fragile dignity in the face of potential violence, and what seemed to some barbarism, both within and without. Against such forces, the deputies try to play a proper part in a great drama, preserving classical decorum against increasing odds.

Ethos

Many of the essential recommendations in the *inventio* section of classical manuals of rhetoric concern the way in which the orator conveys to his public, if possible unobtrusively, an idea of his own qualities. [18] This is normally thought to be particulary important in the opening section of a speech, in which the speaker will attempt, for instance, to appear honest, trustworthy, public-spirited, or modest. In this way the orator's role comes close to the actor's. The two professions had long been linked (Cicero learns from Roscius), and the comparison takes on a new life in the French Revolution, where the protagonists are often seen, by themselves as well as by their enemies, as the actors in a tragic, or sometimes comic, drama.

Sincerity and emotion are the dominant values, at any rate at the period we are concerned with. Eloquence presents itself as the language of the heart. Again and again we hear the tones of eighteenth-century *sensibilité,* the tones of Jean-Jacques above all. Marat is only one of the dozens of deputies who protest 'the purity of [his] heart' (*AP*, 142). Characteristic emotional stances are that of *chaleur*, an ardent zeal for the public good, and horror or indignation ('je fremis.'. 'I shudder. . .') at all that threatens it. So much is virtually universal, and there is no need to dwell on it.

One specific form taken by this shared civic ardour is, of course, the oath, the *serment*. La Harpe wrote of 'the incurable mania for oaths' [19], and in the records of the debates we can easily find notations such as this: 'the whole Assembly is standing, in the attitude of the *serment*' (1 April 1793), reenacting the founding gesture of the Jeu de Paume. Indeed the *serment* is one of the first subjects of discussion on 21 September. One member 'proposes that the Assembly swear an oath to safeguard liberty and equality, or to die defending them' (*AP*, 67). There is an immediate objection, but later in the same day Tallien returns to the charge, calling on the *Conventionnels* to commit themselves with a solemn oath in the presence of the people (the people being of course the spectators in the *tribunes*). But again there are sceptical objections to what could be seen as empty play-acting – 'so many oaths have been violated in the last four years' (*AP*, 70), remarks Basire, who prefers the greater security of penal laws.

Eventually, in this debate about law and order, the proposed *serment* is superseded by a decree. But, on an individual level, many deputies continue to proclaim the same type of commitment in an extreme, often theatrical form. In the proposal just quoted, the deputies were to swear to preserve liberty and equality or die in their defence. In this manner, again and again, speakers proclaim, with greater or lesser sincerity, their willingness to die as martyrs to the cause – a willingness that was all too often to be put to the test. Jean-Claude Bonnet remarks pertinently: 'They all become absolutely sure that they will die in the very act of public speaking; Mirabeau in astonishment discovers the perils of that very act on 28 February 1791 in the Jacobin Club: "I have just passed sentence of death on myself. I'm done for. They'll kill me".' [20] When Marat threatens in a moment of exaltation (or play-acting) to blow his brains out, one may doubt whether he has attained quite the same level of tragic awareness.

Stopping short of self-immolation, many deputies are willing enough to speak of their suffering. This is notably the case with Robespierre. Accused by his numerous enemies of seeking to become a dictator, he is virtually forced to speak of himself and his past behaviour. In doing so, he stresses not only his zeal for the popular cause, but the persecution it has brought on him: 'A man who struggled for so long against all sides with a grim and determined courage, without conciliating anyone, such as man was to be exposed to the hatred and persecution of all ambitious men, all scheming men' (*AP*, 133). This display of self-sacrifice seems like hypocrisy to his opponents, who react with 'laughter and murmurings', but Robespierre turns this to advantage, since it enables him to appear as a Christ, or an Alceste, alone against the laughing Pharisees: 'I demand that those who answer me with laughter, with murmurings, should band together against me, that this little tribunal should sentence me, it will be the most glorious day in my life.'[21] Notice, however, the words 'little tribunal' suggesting that Robespierre, unlike Alceste, is not really alone and that the greater tribunal of the people will avenge him.

Robespierre's stance, perhaps too blatantly adopted, is one of incorruptible courage. Courage, 'manly' courage, is indeed an indispensable virtue, deployed in attack as well as in defence. Citing yet again one of the great model's against whom some at least of the *Conventionnels* measure themselves, Gorsas declares that every deputy is a Brutus (Marcus Brutus on this occasion), and Merlin picks up the hint to present himself as an intrepid patriot: 'I declare that I am ready to stab the first man who would lay claim to the powers of a dictator' (*AP*, 130). Soon after which Danton seems to be measuring himself implicitly against the fortitude of the other Brutus (Voltaire's and David's Lucius Junius), when he declares that he would sacrifice his best friend if he were guilty of unpatriotic designs.

A related ethical *topos* is that of reluctant, but intrepid truth-telling. Here the speaker is not so much pouring out the fullness of his heart as doing his duty, against his humane inclinations (since sensibility and civic virtue should be equally part of the good man's make-up). Various deputies proclaim the duty to speak the truth against the opinions of the majority. So Roland, reporting as Minister of the Interior on the lawless state of the nation, says: 'It would be pointless to elaborate any further on a matter which is repugnant to my heart. But I believed that I had to tell great truths. They concern the salvation of my country; and never has fear stopped my mouth when I believed that my words could be useful' (*AP*, 109).

There is a variant on this on 25 September, in a maiden speech from Maure, who tells his audience how intimidating it is to speak to the Assembly (as indeed it must have been in the Manège): 'Citizens, I mount this rostrum for the first time and I assure you that it is not without emotion that I appear before the representatives of a free and sovereign people. However, vested with the confidence of my fellow citizens, a portion myself of the sovereign power, I could not without crime refrain from speaking the truth to you. I will say to you what Laocoon said to the Trojans. . .' (*AP*, 129). If Marat was Cassandra, here is another figure of the tragic prophet, but combined with that familiar *topos* of the unaccustomed orator. If we leave Laocoon on one side, this is a less dramatic role than that of Brutus. Here the speaker presents himself as the simple, honest fellow who will not, like his opponents, seek to mislead his audience with the tricks of rhetoric. Now some of the *Conventionnels* were not particularly skilled at public speaking (and many of them hardly spoke), but even the most experienced did not disdain this oldest of rhetorical ploys, to which the new situation adds the further attraction of republican virtue and dignity. 'Those who elected us', says Maure,'have not sent us here to unfurl grand phrases and to parade ornate wit' (*AP*,129). Such vanity and frivolity belong to the Ancien Régime.

An interesting example of the 'simple soul' *topos* is to be found in an orator of the opposite camp from Maure, the Girondin Buzot. He had been a deputy at the Constituante, and now voices his Candide-like surprise (not an infrequent rhetorical device) at what he finds on returning to Paris:

> Etranger aux révolutions de Paris, je suis arrivé dans la confiance que je retrouverais ici mon âme indépendante, et que rien ne me ferait sortir de la voie que je m'étais tracée. . .
>
> Je n'appartiens pas à Paris, je n'appartiens à aucun d'eux [the departments], j'appartiens à la République entière. Voilà mon voeu fortement exprimé, malgré les déclamations de ceux qui parlent des Prussiens, de je ne sais quels hommes que je ne connais pas, moi qui vivais paisiblement dans ma province, en cultivant mon âme forte contre toute espèce d'événement. . . (*AP*, 126). [22]

Cincinnatus rather than Laocoon. Speaking at the Jacobins the same night, Fabre d'Eglantine was to mock Buzot's show of provincial innocence.[23] We notice, of course, that he associates honest virtue with the provinces, such declarations being common coin among the anti-Commune speakers – and Danton too does not miss the chance to speak of his provincial origins. Naturally Buzot also proclaims his independence. He belongs to no faction – not Paris, not any particular department, but to 'La République entière'. It has to be said that this is a dubious claim, but it is one that is routinely made by the majority of speakers. As has often been remarked, it is very difficult for the revolutionaries to admit that they represent a specific group rather than France or the Republic or the people as a whole. The Rousseauist ideology of the General Will makes it hard to accept the reality of political division, which is regularly branded as factionalism.

In all that I have so far said about *ethos*, whether it is a question of zeal or of modesty, the stress has been on sincerity, the heart, the emotions. It would be surprising, however, if this were not sometimes countered by a stress on cool reason, the head against the heart. In a setting of extravagance and passion, the role of calm statesman can be an attractive one, and some deputies do indeed make a show of setting logic and philosophical principles against the easy emotions of their opponents. In the five days I have studied, I would not say that this is the dominant mode – though one should not underestimate the amount of plain, down-to-earth, unemotive speaking that did go on during the long days of the Convention. The individual who most clearly wishes to present this image of cool reason is probably Danton. He was, of course, capable of great 'warmth' – his 'de l'audace, encore de l'audace, toujours de l'audace' of 2 September was still ringing in many ears. But when the deputies are plunged in a heated debate about whether judges should be freely elected (which was indeed an incendiary issue), we see him deliberately trying to rise above the fray, avoiding as far as possible any accusation of demagogy: 'I shall reply coldly and without toadying to the people' (*AP*, 86). (He is referring to the ac-accusation by Chasset quoted above.) And indeed this is what he does, at any rate to judge from the reports, adopting a reasoning tone, analysing his opponent's speeches, seeking to base his argument on acceptable philosophical principles. This is a frequent stance with Danton, and it is to be found too in some of the speeches of Marat – contrary to the legendary images.

It seems, however, that the place was not conducive to this type of *ethos*. As Quatremère de Quincy put it, the orator who has to shout is 'ready to become violent'. This auto-intoxication no doubt leads to what seems to a distant reader the excessive and theatrical display of passion, the great and imprudent gestures of tragic self-sacrifice. The *Conventionnels* are playing to a large audience, including as it does the popular galleries, and in this heightened context, there is nothing surprising in their self-projection on the models of Brutus or the Cornelian hero. But one should not forget the tension between heart and head, which we find reflected, when we come to consider oratorical pathos.

Pathos

In a well-known section of his project for public education of 1792, Condorcet, not himself an impressive speaker, had warned of the dangers of passionate oratory. (In doing so, incidentally, he is following in an ancient tradition, as old as rhetoric itself.) [24] He deplores the imitation of models such as Demosthenes, whose primitive emotionalism is not suitable for the present age of reason: 'At that time it was permissable, it was useful even, to move the people; but we owe it to them to educate them... let us then make haste to replace eloquence with reasoning, speakers with books.' [25] In a similar vein, Lequinio, an interesting and little-known figure, exposed all the ways in which the Assembly and the *tribunes* were in fact manoeuvred by unscrupulous speakers.[26] Whether Condorcet liked it or not, however, the appeal to the passions remained an integral part of persuasive oratory in the revolutionary assemblies.

Whose passions? What precisely is the audience that the orator seeks to sway? The 'vous' (and less frequently the 'nous') which figures so often in the speeches refers in the first instance to the 'législateurs', the 'représentants du peuple souverain'. But no doubt the speakers were conscious of a wider public – though less so than in the days of television. They are appealing often to 'La France', for many French people will shortly afterwards be able to read at least a part of the debates in the published form. And most important, they are speaking to the visible representatives of the people, the men and women (but mainly women, it seems) in the *tribunes*. These could be vitally important allies. They could also, it is true, be a nuisance and a danger, but in spite of some deputies' complaints about their conduct, the general view was that they had to be there, that the representatives of the people had to go about their business in the presence of the people. As Volney had put it as early as May 1789, 'We are in the most difficult circumstances; let our fellow citizens surround us on all sides, let them press in upon us, let their presence inspire and animate us'. [27] And press they certainly did!

It is hard from the written record to tell when deputies are playing to the gallery – certainly, to judge from the applause, this was Marat's constant tactic. There were many exhortations to the deputies, usually from Montagnards, to trust the people. This would please the *tribunes*; it may also be calculated to inspire fear in the deputies, as when Collot d'Herbois presses his case with a veiled threat:'No! This law, you will not promulgate it! we have too much faith in the people; and the proof that the laws are always in operation is the fact that the people would dispense justice for themselves if the laws did not dispense justice for them' (*AP*, 125). [28] A mere two weeks after the September massacres, the mention of the 'glaive du peuple' (sword of the people) hanging over the Assembly could be relied on to produce an effect.

At the same time, there is another type of appeal to fear, this time used mainly by the Girondins. This is the evocation of the spectre of anarchy. The state of France, and particularly of Paris, is repeatedly painted in a frightening light, calculated to push the law-abiding, property-owning deputies and their electors to approve punitive laws. So Lasource, on the first day of the Convention, exclaims: 'If the property of each individual was not under the protection of the laws, society would be but the stage for banditry in which the only law would be that of force' (*AP*, 71)

In a situation of real violence, the appeal to fear is natural. It is coupled with what one might cynically call the appeal to vanity, or at least self-respect. Deputies, who may well have felt intimidated by the dramatic theatre in which they found themselves, are constantly being reminded of the grandeur of their mission in language which ressembles that of a Cornelian or Racinian confident trying to bring his vacillating master up to the mark.[29] In his welcoming speech on behalf of the outgoing assembly, François de Neufchâteau had set the tone: 'Fulfill o Representatives the great things to which you have been called..' and Pétion, the President of the new assembly, replies in kind (*AP*, 68). Others will call the Convention an 'assemblée de philosophes' (an assembly of philosophers), and Danton will more than once urge his listeners to rise 'to the level of the great questions' (*AP*, 84). Alternatively, speakers attempt to shame their audience. Robespierre, trying to gain a hearing, appeals to an elementary sense of justice, and Marat taunts provocatively: 'Si vous n'êtes pas à la hauteur, tant pis pour vous' (If you are not up to it, too bad for you) (*AP*, 139). The point is to persuade the *Conventionnels* that the eyes of the world ('l'univers') are upon them as they set about their task. As Danton puts it, 'il faut que l'ennemi sache que la Convention nationale existe' (*AP*, 119) (the enemy must know that the National Convention exists).

The object of such exhortations varies, but one of the commonest is to show strength. The orator shows himself to be manly (the word 'mâle': *virile* is ubiquitous) and the deputies are urged to follow his example, to dare to act, to be worthy of their station. So Danton, with Valmy fresh in the minds of his hearers, declares 'We must appear terrible' (*AP*, 112). A less well-known *Conventionnel*, Osselin, speaks in similar tones against feeble hesitation (the issue being the way to treat an apparently treacherous general): 'This uncertain course is quite unfitting in a National Assembly. Such conduct would denote a weakness, and a faintheartedness which is unworthy of it' (*AP*, 116).

Now this praiseworthy decisive action is often supposed to be based on unanimous feeling, and it is this feeling which orators seek to generate and use. The deputies should be unanimous among themselves, and at one with the whole of the French people, sharing with them emotions of horror, indignation, faith and so on. The deputy Mathieu, pressing for an oath of fidelity early on 21 September, urges: 'Yes, Citizens, I demand that – without discussion – uniquely from the force of sentiment... you swear to be faithful to the nation' (*AP*,71). The words 'without discussion' are essential here. Discussion is replaced by a common impulse.

A fine example of this is provided by the abolition of the monarchy (*AP*, 73-74). This is proposed without much of a preamble by Collot d'Herbois, whose words are greeted by 'unanimous applause'. Some doubts are expressed however, and Grégoire returns to the charge with some vehement eloquence, appealing to the audience's passions of hate and indignation against 'des races dévorantes qui ne vivaient que de chaire humaine', (voracious races which lived on human flesh alone). Whereupon 'l'Assemblée entière se lève par un mouvement spontané , et décrète par acclamation la proposition de M. Grégoire' (the whole Assembly, in one spontaneous movement, stands up and decrees by acclamation M. Grégoire's proposal). Even then, Basire, deputy of the Côte d'Or, attempts to cool things: 'One can but applaud this sentiment which is so much in tune with that of the entirety of the French people. But it would be a frightening example for the people to see an Assembly of philosophers, entrusted with its dearest interests, deliberating in a moment of enthusiasm.'[30] While welcoming the fictitious universality of feeling, he argues that this is not enough for an assembly of law-givers. But he loses. There is no dicussion; as Grégoire says, 'What need is there to discuss when every one is in agreement.'

Exhilarating as this is, it is a dangerous precedent for parliamentary debate, as certain deputies point out on the days following. Attempting to stem the tide, they (and in particular the more 'moderate' members), urge rational discussion as a check on the rapidity of feeling. Thus on 22 September, as Danton is pressing the Convention for a quick decision on the question of the election of judges, Kersaint proposes that this be referred to the Committees, where it can be properly considered. He puts it in this way: 'It is absolutely essential that we should not become embroiled in the discussion of something so important as the matter which has been put to you before we have a hard and fast rule for our debates. We must be on our guard against eloquence, if we do not want to be led by those orators who would be skilful enough to carry us along with them. We must be on our guard against our own passions, and give the people an earnest of our caution' (*AP*, 86).The 'hard and fast rule' is proposed as a much-needed brake on a machine that can easily run out of control. In vain, Sergent, one of the Parisian deputies, denies the need for caution 'when it comes to declaring truths that are engraved in everyone's hearts'- and it is such a truth that judges should be elected by popular vote.

Again we see the power of the Rousseauist model of unanimity. The deputies desire to be seen to speak for the whole nation, for the General Will as popularly understood. A great deal of the oratorical *pathos* of their speeches is devoted to creating this unanimity. The perorations, in particular, seek to transcend debate in the kind of unity of feeling that the great *fêtes* were meant to embody and to create. As a model for the proceedings of a parliament, the *fête* is more than dubious. It may work for the almost festive abolition of the monarchy, but thereafter it can only partially mask the real divisions in the house.

Perhaps what emerges most clearly from the study of these debates is the difficulty, in the circumstances of September 1792 and in the unauspicious setting of the Manège, of keeping a proper control on parliamentary proceedings. We have seen the excitement communicated by speakers to audience, the display of extravagent emotion, the tragic role-playing, the appeal to passion. Quatremère de Quincy, criticising the physical conditions in the hall, had pointed out how deputies, being forced to shout, were led into a violence which spread through the assembly. Such violence, or enthusiasm, used by all parties, could be a powerful means of persuasion, but a dangerous one. We have seen the efforts of many of the *Conventionnels* to curb it by an appeal to old decorum, a demand for a proper order of proceeding or a stress on cool reason. In the last quarter of 1792, this was un uphill struggle

NOTES

1 Having been neglected, this subject is now attracting more attention. Among recent work, see H.U. Gumbrecht, *Funktionen parlementarischer Rhetorik in der französischen Revolution*, Munich, 1978; Lynn Hunt, 'The Rhetoric of Revolution in France', *History Workshop Journal*, 15 (1983), pp. 78–94; J.-C Bonnet, 'La Sainte Masure', in *La Carmagnole des Muses*, edited by J.-C Bonnet and P. Roger, Paris, 1988, pp. 185–222 and in particular, for a clear account of the conditions of speech and the workings of the assemblies, Patrick Brasart, *Paroles de la Révolution: les assemblées parlementaires,* Paris, 1988.

2 On the theory of eloquence during the Revolution, in addition to the works cited above, see A. Aulard, *Les Orateurs de l'Assemblée Constituante*, Paris, 1882, and *Les Orateurs de la Législative et de la Convention*, 2 vols., Paris, 1885–6; also P. Trahard, 'Le Recours à l'eloquence' in his *La Sensibilité révolutionnaire* , Paris, 1936, pp. 175–92.

3 R. Garaudy, *Les Orateurs de la Révolution française*, Classiques Larousse, Paris, 1939.

4 P. France, 'Eloquence révolutionnaire et rhétorique traditionnelle: étude d'une seance de la Convention', *Saggi e ricerche di letteratura francese*, 24 (1985), pp. 143–76.

5 On this question see Aulard, *Orateurs de l'Assemblée Constituante* and France, 'Eloquence révolutionnaire'.

6 See in particular the editions of Danton's speeches by A. Fribourg, (Paris, 1910) and the *Oeuvres complètes* of Robespierre (Paris, 1950–67).

7 References to the *Archives Parlementaires* (*AP*) are to vol. 52 (Paris, 1897) unless otherwise indicated. The relevant volume of the *Reimpression de l'Ancien Moniteur* (Paris, 1840) is vol. XIV.

8 B. Kazansky, 'Rech Lenina', *LEF*, 5 (1924); this volume contains a very interesting set of studies of Lenin's eloquence by the principal Russian formalist critics.

9 L.-S. Mercier, *Le Nouveau Paris*, nouvelle edition, Paris, 1862, vol. I, pp. 275–80, 'Sur la Convention et son style'.

10 Pétion, newly elected President of the Convention, declared on 21 September: 'Nous ne perdron jamais de vue que nous tenons dans nos mains les destinées d'un grand peuple, du monde entier et des races futures' (*AP*, 68) (We shall never lose sight of the fact that we are holding the destiny of a great people, of the whole world and of future races in our hands).

11 David Williams, *Incidents in my Life*, ed. P.France, Brighton, 1980, p. 27. On the make-up of the Convention, see Lynn Hunt, *Politics, Culture, and Class in the French Revolution,* University of California Press, 1984, ch. 5.

12 Quoted by Brasart, *Paroles de la Révolution*, p.84.

13 See *Moniteur*, vol. XX, p. 662.

14 On this question and on many other matters concerning the language of the French Revolution, see F. Brunot, *Histoire de la langue française*, vol. X, Paris, 1939, in particular, on 'langue noble et langue basse', pp. 161–237.

15 (*Renewed murmurings*)
Robespierre: 'When the Assembly no longer wishes to hear me, it will tell me its will. I feel that it is most unfortunate for me to be continually interrupted.
A number of deputies: Get to the point
Robespierre: I will *not* get to the point. Well, I'll force you to listen to me. . .'.

16 'With this continual toadying to the people, we would be entrusting its future to the discretion of a man who had usurped its confidence; this is toadying, I repeat.
Danton: You were not toadying to the people when we did the review. (*Prolonged murmurings*)
Masuyer: I demand that M. Danton be called to order, and reminded what he owes to himself, to the majesty of the people, and to the National Convention.
The President: I can understand that the Assembly, deeply conscious of the air of dignity which must reign over its proceedings, should see

with distress that they are being debased by scandalous exchanges. Let us make it our imperative rule never to allow ourselves any personal abuse.'

17 On this and other related questions see the useful book of P.D.G. Thomas, *The House of Commons in the Eighteenth Century,* Oxford, 1971.

18 The essential source, for this and for *pathos*, is Aristotle's *Rhetoric*.

19 See Hunt, '*The Rhetoric of Revolution*', p. 82.

20 Bonnet, '*La Sainte Masure*', p.215.

21 The reference to Moliere's Alceste is a very frequent one during this period. In Fabre d'Eglantine's comedy *Le Philinte de Molière* (1790), the tables are turned, the moderate Philinte being seen as the real misanthrope, whereas the virtuous Alceste emerges as positive hero. This was of course the way Rousseau put the matter in his *Lettre à d'Alembert sur les spectacles*.

22 'A stranger to the revolutionary events in Paris, I arrived confident that here I would find again the independence of my soul and that nothing would cause me to leave the path that I had traced for myself... I do not belong to Paris, I belong to none of them [the departments], I belong to the entire Republic. That is my vow strongly expressed despite the ranting of those who speak about the Prussians, about indeterminate men whom I do not know, I who was living peaceably in my province cultivating the strength of my soul against any possible event...'
The *Moniteur* gives a somewhat different text according to which Buzot says: 'j'y conserverai mon âme indépendante' (I shall maintain the independence of my soul) and 'moi qui vivait au sein de ma retraite, dans mon département' (I who was living deep within my retreat, in my departement).

23 See P.-J.-B Buchez and P.-C Roux, *Histoire parlementaire de la Révolution Française*, Paris, 1835, vol.XIX, p.70.

24 On this question see P. France, *Rhetoric and Truth in France, Descartes to Diderot,* Oxford, 1972.

25 Condorcet, *Procès-verbaux du Comité d'Instruction Publique de l'Assemblée Législative*, pp. 200–3.

26 See Bonnet, '*La Sainte Masure*', p.200–2.

27 Quoted by Brasart, '*Paroles de la Révolution*' p.31.

28 Here again the *Moniteur* gives an interestingly different version: instead of 'nous avons trop de confiance...' we read: '*vous* devez avoir confiance dans la justice du peuple'. (*you* must have faith in the people's justice).

29 That the deputies might not feel so sure of their eminence is suggested by the sort of mockery we find in this counter-revolutionary song: 'Comme ils sont faits!/Cela fait pitié, je vous jure/ Comme ils sont faits!/On les prendrait pour des jokais/Ils en ont la tournure/L'accoutrement et la coiffure/ Comme ils sont faits!' (God what a sight!/ It fills you with pity in faith/ God what a sight!/ You'd take them for jockeys/ They've got just the look/ the rig and the hair cut/ God what a sight!)

30 The words 'de philosophes' are missing from the *Moniteur*'s account of this speech.

ROUND TABLE DISCUSSION

Bert HALSALL commented that what Peter France had presented, by way of illustration for his paper, had been an analysis of certain speeches and declarations made in the Convention, but wondered whether he might not now give closer attention to their power to carry conviction because – to the modern listener – they sounded rather obvious and simple. What, for example, had been their level of eloquence? of pathos? of hyperbole? How had the physical surroundings of the Assembly influenced revolutionary rhetoric in general? What had been new in that eloquence? How, in short, had the content of the speeches combined with their powers to convince? Peter FRANCE agreed that the question of credibility, within the context of the Convention, ought to be looked at as a priority and with all due seriousness because it was 'tempting to look upon these and similar speeches with what has been called "the immense condescension of the present to the past". It is all too easy to slip into a type of good-taste mockery (of the hyperbole in particular, which is the vulgar figure of all vulgar figures)'. Peter France went on to further preface the coming general debate on the above problems by explaining that one of the difficulties of examining revolutionary eloquence lay in the fact that –though at work in a *new* situation –it was 'difficult to pinpoint elements in the eloquence itself which were themselves new and any different from the eloquence as recorded and analysed in previous centuries. One is *not* talking about anything that represents a new way of speaking, although it is only right to point out that the new *situation* placed a tourniquet on the *old* way of speaking to the extent that the new bottles created, as it were, a new wine'. Nelly WILSON, picking up, as a supplementary issue, the question of personal abuse, wondered how the *Conventionnels* had reacted to this problem and whether they differentiated between individual attacks on people whom they saw as a living embodiment of certain ideas and policies, and attacks which were merely slanderous. Peter FRANCE agreed that we had to see a difference between crude insult (which had not been acceptable according to official decorum) and those 'harsh' references to people in a critical way which had been seen as a proper and frank way of proceeding. 'The training which any of these people would have had in rhetoric would have been Cicero; and Cicero on Catiline, as the classical model, allows for ample recourse to *personality*. Since so much of the rhetoric used in the Convention is *forensic* – having to do with accusation and defence – *personality* is bound to play a central role'. Philippe ROGER said that 'this method of attack had been closely linked in practice with the *ad hominem* argument which, as Nelly Wilson suggests, was an attempt to personify the argument in the speaker. But I feel that this particular problem was, within context, part of that more general debate on the public accusation of individuals which had surfaced rather noisily in 1790 with Mirabeau and the question of *délation* (denunciation), which is the most extreme form of *ad hominem* attack. Mirabeau had launched the idea that denunciation was the duty of the citizens of the new France; and this particular word – which had had much more negative connotations until then – provoked an on-going debate. It was like the debate on calumny which took place just after Thermidor. But, returning to the main problem (i.e. the revolutionary power to convince), I wonder whether there are not three overlapping concepts of oratorical eloquence, the first is the traditional type of *discours académique*, or what we can call the oratorical art as literature. This is a tradition which bogs down parliamentary debate for some good time; for example, the Girondins were much attacked on the grounds that their discourse was too ornate, that they made "commemorative columns" out of their emotions. The devotees of the ornate style will meet more and more resistance from 1792 onwards, and their ornateness is an argument used against them. The second type is eloquence as pure energy, though here I think that you have to differentiate between those deputies who wrote their speeches and those who did not. The third type – and here I am thinking of Robespierre and Saint-Just – is the idea of the *morceau oratoire* as a *morceau de philosophie*. By this I mean a written, moral contribution which reposes essentially upon the "intangibility of the written".' Peter FRANCE was not too happy with the so-called 'philosophical' category nor with the rather rigid schematisation. 'If indeed a large number of speeches in the Convention *were* read, one is struck by the sheer number which are not *morceaux oratoires* and which are not "pure energy" either. I think that we are probably too inclined to underline the great speeches of the Dantons, the Vergniauds and the Robespierres, because the ordinary use of the word in the Convention is with people who have something to say and who say it as quickly as possible. There is then a *utility* or *necessary* discourse which fills out much of the time and which is a sort of background noise.'

Asked by Alain BOURDON whether there had been a theoretical debate on rhetoric itself within the Assembly, Peter FRANCE said that rhetoric was mentioned as such in some speeches. It was also broached, for example, in Condorcet's report to the Committee on Education; but even in the archives of the latter, little is to be found on rhetoric as a topic. 'I wonder whether its presence and its use appeared self-evident..or unnecessary, because from time to time you find someone like Lequinio, the Montagnard, who says that we do not need rhetoric, that saying what we have to say is sufficient. So, in sum, there *are* remarks here and there, but nothing which approaches a developed debate or a serious, sustained investigation'. John RENWICK added that concern with rhetoric in the various Assemblies of the revolutionary period had essentially been concern with rhetoric or eloquence as *seduction*. 'The first expression of worry can be found with Mounier and the Monarchiens who, in the first days of the Revolution, wanted two Chambers, on the English model, in order to ensure that an orator, or a series of orators working in the same direction, could not bewitch one Assembly and turn it around despite its and the nation's own "best interests". It is also the concern of Condorcet (in the report just mentioned by Peter France) who is specifically anxious to guard against impassioned, siren-song eloquence. Even Mirabeau himself, who knows the power of the spoken word better than most, warns against the way in which impassioned, exalted language can be used to justify imprudent policies or actions. This is a common worry, which is there in the background all the time.' Peter FRANCE: 'Yes, it is often a worry that you express when you are losing or facing an up-hill struggle. One of the traditional points of rhetoric is to say: "do not listen to that orator, do not follow that pied piper". The most interesting text that I have seen in this respect is the one quoted by Bonnet ['La Sainte Masure' in *La Carmagnole* pp.200–2]. It is a text taken from Lequinio [*Les Préjuges détruits*, 1792] who –without apparently wanting it to seem like a root-and-branch condemnation of eloquence –shows the way in which you can manipulate the galleries and the Assembly.' John RENWICK added that this manipulation had become 'tragically evident to the Girondins in the course of 1793, so tragically evident that they decided to use the forthcoming transfer of the Convention from the Salle du Manège to the Salle des Machines (May-June 1793) as their opportunity to make an attack on the composition of the four public galleries which tended always to be full of Parisian supporters of the Montagne. Until August 1792, two of those galleries had been reserved for spectators with official invitations, particularly from the provinces. The proposal made by the Gironde was that the Convention go back to the old system; that was accepted (13 May 1793), but within a week the Montagne had counter-attacked and a rather nasty skirmish took place (18 May) when a large (renta-)crowd of *Parisiennes* terrorised and turned away the people arriving at the Convention with official invitations .. from the Gironde.'

Siân REYNOLDS took up these various references to the appeal made, in particular, to the Sans-culottes and the galleries – and the attempts to manipulate them – to raise another aspect of the problem: how to define the rapport between the people in the public galleries and the deputies? 'Sometimes the speakers, the Girondins for example, complain that they have been tyrannized for too long by the galleries; at other times orators, will quite deliberately say –particularly in Versailles at the beginning –that they are in the presence of the people'. Peter FRANCE felt that appealing to the people was not just a question of tactics, of getting oneself valorised by them. 'There was a genuine feeling that the deputies must be in the presence of the people. It is not the mere crude ploy of using the immediate representatives of the people as your vehicle for winning. My impression is that, with the deputies from 1789 onwards, a feeling of democracy implies *glasnost*, implies visibility. But much depends upon *whom* you are visible to. Because the composition of the public galleries changes rapidly and radically. Those sitting there during the Constituant Assembly are by no means the same as those under the Convention'. Siân REYNOLDS, referring back to Lynn Hunt's examination of the political activity of women (1789–93) [see pp. 34-35] and to John Renwick's just having mentioned their role in the attack on the Gironde, commented on the overwhelming female presence in the public galleries and said that 'Dominique Godineau's book [*Citoyennes tricoteuses*] – which is full of examples showing that the large numbers of people who had become unemployed by the collapse of the luxury trade were women – explains why this should be so. But, of course, the clear message is that women are used as legitimising forces in some circumstances and not in others. They are not *citoyennes à part entière* (full citizens).' Peter FRANCE quoted evidence to suggest that the proportion of women in the galleries could be as high as nine out of ten. 'But I have never seen any recognition of this fact in the oratory. There is, however, another form of female presence in the Assembly, and these are the deputations to the bar. Or they can just as well be delegations of women, who are also allowed to speak and to process'. Eric WALTER referred to deputations of women 'who had presented to the Assembly written addresses which often seem not to be theirs. Once again we are in all probability faced with another type of manipulation. They were either being used or allowing themselves to be used'. Peter FRANCE (agreeing generally with John RENWICK's comment that, though one could sense manipulation in certain situations, it was very difficult to prove), referred people however to his earlier investigation [see note 4] into one day in the life of the Convention (10 April 1793). That day had begun precisely with the use of a deputation and a petition (probably attributable to Marat) and had become an interesting and complicated battle between Gironde and Montagne in which one could see the outlines of manipulation more clearly. But he conceded that the evidence is often not so clear.

Philippe ROGER said that it would be an enormous task to reconstitute the composition of that public (or those successive publics); but he saw this as a problem which overlapped with a problem that Lynn HUNT had raised informally and which she felt had to be discussed, and this was the question of unanimity and the search for unanimity. 'From the very beginning, in Versailles, there is the slow creation of a mythology of fusion with the people. We have an interesting account of this from Etienne Dumont [*Souvenirs sur Mirabeau*] who describes the problems that the National Assembly met in its early meetings – just after it had proclaimed itself *National* – due to the permanent intervention of the public..not in order to pressurise, but out of sheer effervescence, effusiveness. They mix with the deputies, they chatter incessantly. In the beginning there is then disorder, even total confusion. But Mirabeau opposed several attempts to police the Chamber and opposed them on the grounds that the physical presence of what, for convenience, was called the *people* was the only legitimisation of the work of the Assembly. Indeed, what is interesting at this very early date is that the Assembly has as yet no legitimacy; not only has it no legitimacy, but it is physically threatened by the Court. It is a time of extreme political and symbolical fragility. And I wonder whether it is not this early fragility which is responsible for the discourse of legitimisation which is conducted with constant reference to the fusional and physical co-presence of the people. That people, however, will steadily become a pressure group.'

Lynne HUNT: 'One of the essential problems for the historian is the model of unanimity and the origins of this model, the ways in which it operates, whether it is specific to the dire circumstances such as Peter France described them in late 1792, or whether it is implicit in the revolutionary relationship to language. I say this because the debate which is currently taking shape is going to centre around deciding whether 1789 is the source of everything or not. More precisely I would like to know what gives substance to the voice of the people? How can the voices of the deputies be related to the voice of the people? The issue is whether it is the belief in unanimity which makes the organisation of political life difficult or whether it is a more accidental disorganisation of political life which allows this particular invested mythological view of the voice of the people to arise. I got the impression that Peter France was leaning towards the latter interpretation, that he was saying that the sheer organisational difficulties (problems with thelocale; order of speaking; choice of political structure; empirically worked out principles concerning the presence of the people) resulted in there being a sort of *mythologisation* of the unanimity of the voice of the people. But I think that he also shows that there was incredible uncertainty where this relationship might really lie in terms of a particular speaker. Certainly the deputies understood that who was in the galleries was not *le peuple français* (especially if that public was composed of a large proportion of women). They may have imagined, in self identification, that they were speaking for the people. But the sense in which they *represented* this people is very fragile.' Philippe ROGER agreed that a problem did arise from the notion of representation/representativeness. If there was fragility then it was a fragility which had been profoundly structured by previous discourses and previous political mythologies. 'In the beginning, for example, the deputies were felt to be (and considered themselves to be) totally bound by their "imperative mandate" which they did not have the right to alter. They had been asked to solve a financial crisis, not create a National Assembly. However, even though the force of things had taken them and their successors way beyond this position, a variety of things pointed to there still being deep uncertainty about the status of representation/representativeness'.

In various comments and questions Baldine SAINT-GIRONS, Jennifer BIRKETT and Eric WALTER suggested that a further area for discussion should be the notion of the Assembly as theatre, even charade; the theatricality of gesture and the problem of credibility. Peter FRANCE: 'From time immemorial acting and public speaking have been allied trades; indeed there is nothing new (look at the Cicero-Roscius relationship) about seeing an orator as an actor. What is striking, however, at this time is the presence in people's minds of a very dominant theatrical model: the whole assembly procedure is theatre. But the word must not be seen as denigration: a *theatre* is a place in which you perform, and again *performance* is not a negative term either (performance is what you give of yourself in public). But both can become negative (*charade* is of course one of those words which make it become so) in a certain type of discourse. The latter is mostly seen in Taine (but is still fairly widely employed today). Here the theatrical metaphor is used as a way of saying: this is an epiphenomenon; these people are merely amusing themselves.' Eric WALTER drew attention to the roles of oratory, as opposed to the role of the theatre, under the Ancien Regime. The eloquence of the pulpit and of the bar had been recognised by the monarchy; but the eloquence which had been – or could have been – liberatory had been banned. Hence the theatre became a *philosophical* platform. Within the strict context of the Revolution he had found, however, that the notions of *theatre* and *decorum* were often clearly linked. 'Some people were particularly sensitive about decorum when political events were concerned. Marat denounced the popular demonstrations of 14 July 1792, saying that they were pantaloonery, totally grotesque buffoonery, a political farce. And Robespierre himself – on 5 February 1794 – denounced those who wore the mask of patriotism, the hypocrites, the actors, saying that their insolent parodies disfigured the sublime drama of the Revolution. The theatre is also therefore a degrading metaphor because you can pass from one reference to another, going in opposite directions'. Peter FRANCE : 'The person who states this in the classic way is Marx in the *18th Brumaire*, where he talks about tragedy that repeats itself as farce. But in fact the tragedy does not necessarily *repeat* itself as farce. It is *at one and the same time* both tragedy and farce. It is the notion, which one gets in Yeats, of mask and anti-mask. Or, if you go back to ancient Greece, you will find that –with the tragic trilogy –goes the comedy. Tragedy implies its own anti-tragedy or parody.' Philippe ROGER saw exactly the same sort of reflection, or pattern, in the counter-revolutionary press of 1789–91, which – alluding to the inverse French theatrical practice – often stated that the deputies were playing the comedy before the tragedy. David DENBY thought that the question of theatre and credibility, and of unanimity, joined up with a previous discussion on the *fête* [p. 20]: 'I raised the question of the *fête* and Philippe Roger responded by saying that there had been a dramatic and progressive lack of connection between the increasingly ridiculous *mises en scène* (staging) and the practical reality of the time. It seemed to me that, if you are talking about theatre, one of the things you are talking about is the *fête*, in the sense that it is precisely then that –increasingly as the questions of unanimity and representivity become problematic –you witness this attempt to project unanimity through the *mise en scène*. With hindsight it is easy to see the lack of connection between the script and what was being scripted on the one hand, and what was likely to happen (and did happen) on the other. But, at that time, it is a fact that those who produced the *mises en scène* for the *fête* did, at some level, believe that they were producing a possible representation both of reality and of the people'. Accepting this view, Peter FRANCE added that these *fêtes* and 'in unequal but nevertheless definite measures, carried with them a strong tale of parody and derision. It seems to me that the vulnerability of the high seriousness of the *fête* is exactly paralleled by the vulnerability of parliamentary oratory'. Philippe ROGER: 'During the Revolution, a number of dramatists tried to create a theatre of unanimity, in which the political problems which they believed were worth discussing could be posed. The typical example of this is Jean-Louis Laya's *L'Ami des Lois*; Laya's intention, at that moment when the political crisis was becoming acute, was to ask the question: What do we want? But the theatre which asked questions, which invited debate and reaction was, however, anathema for a Rousseauist who was also a Sans-culotte. The response to his play was so furious that, from then on and as a reaction, theatres staged re-enactments of the great revolutionary events (e.g. the Taking of the Bastille). Or else you find the massive militant intervention of the audience which interrupts both play and actors; and here we are dealing with that sort of fusional desire which Rousseau wanted to put in place of pure representation'. Peter FRANCE: 'In this respect the Assembly, as I described it, is desperately aspiring to the atmosphere and condition of the *fête*. For example, the Tennis Court Oath, the subsequent swearing of oaths in the Assembly is an attempt to become a *fête*, to achieve a unanimity which, of course, is not possible'.

Jean-Piere LACROIX: 'One last question. How many people were there, in 1789 – out of a population of 26–27 million – who had been educated in a way allowing them to speak in public, who were capable of playing a role in this vast drama?' Philippe ROGER: 'The educated section of the population is tiny, something of the order of 40,000-50,000. The orators of the Revolution are, however, not necessarily people who have had training in rhetoric. Many are, of course, over and above their education, orators by profession: they are churchmen or lawyers. But there is a new type of orator (who has no experience of the *art* of oratory) who has exercised a profession to do with the word: the number of actors is high, and this had to do with their ability to perform in public. Neither must you neglect the influence (if you go outside the Assembly) of the various political Clubs. Here there was a vast range of talents, of oratorical energy, among people who are, for the most part, uneducated. There is then a small body of people who have been trained in rhetoric. But what is striking, and what struck the contemporaries (who left us numerous testimonies), is that we are dealing with a *new* oratorical art. Mercier, for example, said that "in 1789 all the dives and cafés imitated the National Assembly, and after 1790 it was the National Assembly which was obliged to imitate them". Mercier was not favourable to this development which he saw as a degradation of the oratorical level of debate. But his remark is interesting because it shows that the generalisation of *public* debate was having such an impact that it was becoming a rhetorical model for the upper Assemblies'.

Five

BABEUF'S CANDOUR: THE RHETORICAL INVENTION OF A PROPHET

Eric Walter

Like a sun in the night (Michelet)

Examining Babeuf's revolutionary eloquence is a paradoxical enterprise. Compared with the 'big names' of the political scene, he never came to the fore as an orator, anywhere really important. As an activist he does not have the stature of a great political writer, like for example Robespierre. Moreover, as a public figure, he appears on the national stage only after the fall of Robespierre himself. But it was then that Babeuf emerged as an energetic pamphleteer and prophet.

I shall say nothing here about Babouvism, its genesis or its evolution. Suffice it to say that, with his Conspiracy of the Equals, Babeuf's essential contribution to Babouvism was to have transformed what had been egalitarian Messianism into a political programme. Catapulted into the Revolution, this old Messianism became secular, was grafted onto the social struggles to be broadcast through oratory and the press. This was to mean a change in its status as discourse. The requirement to 'go public' forced it to invent its own rhetoric of persuasion. With all due respect to the adepts of 'scientific socialism', the power behind the discourse of the Equals is to be attributed, not to a science of historical evolution (even embryonic), but to its ability to respond to a desperate need to *believe*: in 1795–7, preaching the promised land and 'collective happiness'[1] was alone what could assuage the suffering caused by the recent collapse of the people's hope for the future.

My aim is therefore to focus attention on Babeuf the talented publicist, who was foremost an apostle with a power to convince which sprang less from conceptual rigour than from the sheer impulsion that was generated by his messianic phrasing. In approaching this great master of the prophetic discourse, I have relied less on Jaurès (his most attentive reader, but over-concerned to find a place for the 'ideologue' in his socialist Pantheon) than on Michelet. The latter misappreciated Babeuf's doctrine but he got much nearer to its pure ability to make men dream. As he said: '[his] egalitarian mysticism which came to him in his prison dreams [...] was like a sun in the night'.[2]

The outspokenness of the outsider

We must start by asking a series of questions. How did Babeuf become an actor on the political stage? What paths did he follow in establishing himself as a publicist and orator? What stylistic options, what linguistic acts went into the making of his revolutionary discourse? How did Babeuf invent his text and was he himself invented by that text? Answering these questions means apprehending the relationship between Babeuf's cultural trajectory, his political itinerary and his rhetorical strategies (Michelet speaks pertinently about 'his writing campaigns').

In certain respects the path taken by this self-educated man is not unlike the paths that were followed by Rousseau, Jamerey-Duval, Prion or Ménétra.[3] What strikes one about this plebeian ('I was born in the gutter') is the tension that existed between his requirement to be free and his dependency on his chosen mediators. On the one hand, there is the voracious reader with avid, unmethodical pretensions to encyclopaedic knowledge. But, on the other, there is the cultural outsider who for long needed spiritual fathers to legitimise his intellectual gains. The master-apprentice relationship which he created (then destroyed) with Dubois de Fosseux stood him in stead of school, salon and learned society. But how should one interpret the complex relationship which he maintained with Coupé in 1791? and others later on? Despite the originality of his ideas did this former *scribe feudiste* feel himself, culturally, to be an 'equal' only in 1794–7 when he was conversing with Buonarroti and Germain? At all events there is a striking contrast between Babeuf and the early-gained independence of people such as Marat, Saint-Just and Robespierre (who were all, it is true, bourgeois products of the colleges).

His political itinerary betrays a similar paradox. His career as a militant (1789–97), more than a third of which is spent in different prisons, can mainly be seen in three phases. First, in Picardy, Babeuf the activist plays an outstanding role in the rural revolution and arouses the interest of Marat. This encourages him to launch his first newspaper: *Le Correspondant picard*.[4] Then, in Paris, he is to be found strategically placed in the urban revolution, working for Chaumette, helping to administer the supply of food. Finally, after Thermidor, he quickly gained a powerful reputation as an orator and publicist by swimming – on the far Left – with the Thermidorian current and then by plunging into the opposing current and becoming all at once the publicist, the theoretician, the educator and the arbiter of that new type of faction which was to be baptised the Conspiracy of the Equals. Yet, if we disregard those last two years of his life, we must say that, politically and culturally, Babeuf for long remained on the fringes of the various centres of power, dependent on his dissimilar protectors. As an often unemployed copyist, as a half-starved intellectual with a family to support, as a publicist of originality but who was devoid of any backing at all, Babeuf had – more than once – to go looking for patrons: some (such as Coupé) were estimable but disappointing, others (such as Chaumette) were more powerful but tortuous, others again (such as Fournier 'the American') were dubious, while finally others (such as Tallien, and Fréron, and then – until January 1795 – Fouché himself) were dangerous.

We must not, however, deduce from this that Babeuf's intellectual independence was unavoidably diminished. Everything proves the opposite. Being socially *déclassé*, culturally an outsider and politically a hybrid, Babeuf would always have been destined for minority activism and doctrinal isolation. As R. Andrews' sociography of the Conspiracy testifies,[5] those three characteristics are to be found in the collective biography of the Equals in 1796.

Such a milieu was particularly favourable to the emergence of a polemical and prophetic discourse directed against the government. By proclaiming themselves – in the name of the 'real' people – the harbingers of a people to come (the glorious people of the 'Equals'), Babeuf, Germain and Maréchal occupy, within discourse, a position which had been deserted since the liquidation of the *Enragés*. That position and that discourse were those of millenarian prophecy, along with its enunciative and figurative strategies, its argumentative processes, its own distinctive phrasing and rhythms.

It is unusual that a militant like Babeuf, after his successes in the provinces, either could not or would not develop those inner dispositions which might have made of him a statesman. But this inability has, as its correlative, what I propose to call a 'candour', the candour of an *ingénu* (who is both a modest man and a megalomaniac), who asserted that he was totally open (cf. the last issue of the *Tribun du peuple*, in which he declared that he was preparing an exploit 'of naked force'). Unlike Danton and Mirabeau, men of action 'who could speak with two tongues' (F. Furet), unlike Robespierre or Saint-Just who mixed invocation of principle with political manoeuvring, Babeuf needs to utter all he believes and, above all, to believe all he utters: hence, in his rhetorical presentation of self, that Rousseauistic 'ethos' of sincerity which requires as much value to be accorded to the authenticity of what one is saying as to the force of truth behind one's ideas. Not unlike Desmoulins in 1793, but in a more simplistic way, Babeuf wishes both to *speak true*, be true (foremost in his own eyes), and *speak the truth*, i.e. proffer a discourse of authority, a discourse which eyes political power, in short: a *political* discourse. But, being at pains to attest the purity of his intentions, Babeuf's polemical and political discourse tends to be contained within another which is ethical and prophetic. It is the combination of these two types of discourse which makes for the mystery of his writings as for the different ways in which they can be read.[6]

Words, power, blood: the discourse of sacrifice

Never were lives and/or one's own life narrated with such frequency as between the Terror and Thermidor. In a climate which, at its direst, reminds one of Rousseau's *Dialogues*, the autobiographical deposition is the outcome of current circumstances: the journalist, the orator, the militant, the suspect in the presence of his judges, the accused person in prison (Brissot, Mme. Roland), all recapitulate their lives, reply to the accusations laid against them, rediscovering, in the process, the principle of *ethos* in rhetoric itself which requires the subject to make a clear display of his sincerity, of his public and private virtues. But the urgency of the situation gives a dramatic flavour to the way in which people project themselves. Civic religiosity means that the sacrifice which is demanded from individuals in the sacred name of the People, or the Country or Humanity becomes more demanding. But above all there is the gesture of *self*-sacrifice (Marat, for example, offering his life for the salvation of the people) which justifies the call on other people to sacrifice their own lives but which also legitimises suspicion, denunciation, trial and purge.[7]

In a time of Terror, the rhetoric of sacrifice falls into that megalomania of radical regeneration that Hegel diagnosed as being 'raving presumptuousness'.[8] Babeuf analysed and denounced the danger of such presumptuousness. His own conception and practice of sacrifice show that he was poles apart from the terrorists of 1793–4. And if refusing to shed the blood of your fellow man is artless then Babeuf was so in a variety of ways which are worth examining.

The first thing to notice is his notion and practice of paternity. With Babeuf, the 'name of the father' crystallises an ideal of self which is morally binding on both the militant and the private individual. From his writings there emerge three different types of father figure, all to be situated in the domain of sacrifice. The first is the tender-hearted individual who is torn between the call to militancy and the urgency of his family's straitened circumstances. Whether writing to his wife or his sons, he pours out an unfailing tenderness which would have love of family and love of humanity combined: 'Bonjour gueux, mon coquinot, mon petit homme, mon ami, mon cousin, mon camarade' (Hello scamp, my little rascal, my little man, my friend, my kinsman, my comrade).[9] The same ambition galvanises Babeuf the educator who is as concerned about the progress made by his sons as he is eager to preach the good word to his readers, to the broad family of the Equals. (It is this hope in regeneration which animates Babeuf, even in prison, quite unlike Marat who was often reduced to crying in the wilderness without even the hope of having posterity). And this mythology of paternity culminates in a third figure: the sacrificed saviour, the martyred father...a fate which Babeuf had accepted some time before. On 17 April 1793, he had consoled his destitute family with a grandiose hope: 'I hope to show them a father that the whole world will look upon as the Saviour of mankind'.[10] In Vendôme, on 27 May 1797, the whole display of his own blood freely shed through an act of suicide gives a brilliant aura to the testament of a martyr who, unlike the Montagnard leaders, was never in a position to dispense death himself. In the grand stoic manner of heroic suicide, he proclaims the founding faith of a father, an apostle and a prophet who is temporarily vanquished but who will live on in his sons, in all those who will share his dreams.

In refusing to shed blood, but in coming face to face with examples of savagery born of action, Babeuf will lay himself open to all sorts of contradictions. His engagement in the peasant struggles (1790–1) confirms him in the belief that popular violence fomented by centuries of oppression is legitimate. And, on the question of regicide, we can suppose that he was in sympathy with Saint-Just's belief such as Michelet briefly defines it: 'his [Louis XVI's] blood was the sign, the test, the fatal *shibboleth* by which alone the patriots were to be recognized'.[11] And yet, the man who admired in Marat 'the plebeian pen' showed no sympathy for the appeals made by the 'Ami du peuple' for preventive executions and resolutely spoke out against state terror, whether it was Jacobin or absolutist. Without seeking to find in his writings the elements of a theory of political violence, we can however point to certain indications of his instinctive and reasoned horror when faced with what he chose to call 'égorgerie' (butcherisery). In a letter to his wife (23 July 1789), there is a commentary on the decapitation of Foulon and Berthier after the fall of the Bastille:

> Oh, how I found their joy painful! I was both satisfied and dissatisfied, I said so much the better and so much the worse. I can

> understand that the people should dispense justice for themselves, I approve of that justice when it is satisfied by the annihilation of the guilty, but today, how could it be other than cruel? The ultimate penalties of all sorts, quartering, torture, the wheel, the stake, the whip, gibbets, public executioners here, there and everywhere have given us such bad moral principles! Our masters, instead of giving us orderly government, made us into barbarians because they are so themselves. They are reaping and they shall reap what they have sown, for all this, my poor wife, will – it seems – have terrible repercussions: this is just the beginning.[12]

What, in 1989, is interesting about his remarkable interpretation is the accurate appreciation of the gap that existed between the political modernity of the event itself and the tenacious old-fashioned nature of the mentalities behind it. But when dealing with spilt blood, Babeuf is not always so clear: it is very difficult to discern a coherent analysis of the Terror in that tireless indictment which, in September 1794, he develops in the *Journal de la liberté de la presse*.

The same confusion pervades that brilliant and weird pamphlet which he wrote in December 1794, entitled: *Le Système de dépopulation*.[13] His thesis is brutally simple: the reason for the war in the Vendée, he claims, is that Robespierre thought up a plan for solving the problem of foodstuffs by widespread extermination. With its torrential eloquence, this text breathlessly communicates the vertigo experienced by Thermidorian France, caught unawares by the ordeal of that guilt-inducing rememoration which Michelet compared to 'a gigantic dantesque poem'.[14] In it, Babeuf skilfully plays several different roles and registers: first he is a fierce but impartial investigator, then a moving witness of Vendéan bereavement while, finally, he is the apostle of a fraternity among Frenchmen which has to be rebuilt. I note also the intensity of his exclamatory style: to describe the horror of the situation, Babeuf either mobilises strong images or (in a sort of hyperbolical effervescence) seeks to convey the impression of a paroxysm with his frequent use of convulsive neologisms, for example: *égorgerie* (butcherisery), *massacrades* (massacrades), *carnassité* (carnivorousity), *furorisme* (furyism), etc.... I note again the way in which he highlights the oratorical snares that underwrote the Terror, denouncing the excessive power that had been generated by 'civic frenzy', the crimes that had been pre-exonerated by decrees with 'harsh and atrocious forms' and the killers who had been 'electrified' by 'utterances of frenzied enthusiasm'. In a word, hallucinated and incantatory, Babeuf's text blends Thermidor's dire imagining of a 'populicide' holocaust with the expression of ancestral fears: conspiracy and deliberate starvation.

His pamphlet is essentially explicable by the circumstances. Babeuf was then in prison, dependent on Fouché, who perhaps got him to produce this indictment of 'the crimes of Carrier': the trial of the butcher of Nantes, now the scape-goat, gave the ex-terrorists the opportunity to launder their past.[15] But, paradoxically, Babeuf quotes at length from Carrier's self-defence, thus giving an eloquent picture of the atrocities that could be imputed to the Vendéans themselves; paradoxically, he does not spare those who oversaw the Terror and, paradoxically, he turns against the interests of the man who supposedly got him to write in the first place.

Highly motivated in affective terms, Babeuf's rejection of bloody violence will, however, prove to be strategically untenable. Late in 1794 – on his neo-Robespierrist tack – he starts moving towards an about-face. And one year later (Michelet, in some disappointment, calls this Babeuf's 'being brutally swept along by logic'), he finally legitimises the alliance between the Equals and the remaining Montagnards, sacrificing the memory of Chaumette to an apology for Robespierre. And yet his justification for the September massacres (*Tribun du Peuple*, no. 40, February 1796) is more Maratist than Jacobin. It partakes of the military view of a conspiracy which envisages necessarily violent seizure of power: first, ineluctable popular revenge, then the 'provisional' dictatorship of the 'insurrectory Directory' (*Directoire insurrecteur*). These virtuous exercises in violence are sacrifices which must be accepted before man can attain 'collective happiness'.[16]

We must also see the question of sacrifice from one final angle: Babeuf's reflexion on 'the empire of words'. His candour once again allowed him to say what, in politics, is known and is done (without being discussed). An assiduous reader, even before 1789, of Domergue's *Journal de la langue française*, Babeuf used its debates on political eloquence as grist to his own inquiry. Speculating on the representational function of language, he criticised tyrannical, metaphysical abstraction, opposing to it the robust linguistic clarity of the woodcutter or the carpenter. He developed, with the help of Domergue, an indictment of 'the abuse of words' in political discourse, formulating a critique of political passions which came down to revealing, in the discourse of power, the perverse workings of the spirit of domination. In short, according to Babeuf, demagogues manipulate things and men by their arcane use of 'hollow, meaningless words'.

Brought to maturity by three years of Revolution, Babeuf's ideas were publicly applied to the events of September 1794 when he devoted the majority of his *Journal de la liberté de la presse* to a stubborn critique of Jacobin language, and (mainly) of the formula 'the revolutionary government' (a talisman-phrase that had urgently to be destroyed if they wished to be free from the illegitimate power of the survivors of Robespierrism). Babeuf energetically analyses the Terror as a malady of the public spirit which had – among other things – disfigured the 'simple' language of the grand principles:

> They expressed, in an obscure jargon, in an unintelligible new-coined language, views which were quite *eversive* of public liberty; they perfected the art of Machiavelli so as to bring the people to the point where they paid no further attention to their sovereign rights, and believed [...] that to be sure of their liberty they had to start by renouncing it'.[17]

Hence the theme (not unlike the ultimate proposals made by Camille Desmoulins) that France can emerge from the Terror only through linguistic re-education; reconstructing the civil compact requires a clean sweep of 'the new language of political abstractions' in order to re-instate 'a simple language': 'the free idiom of democratism'. Six weeks later – on 13 October 1794 – there appeared that famous address (which will mean imprisonment for Babeuf), that fiery worded tally of the crimes of the Terror which challenged the verbal intimidation of those who still defended their 'infamous government' by claiming that it had saved the Republic:

> Do not point to the thing any more than to the word. Disguised behind a golden name, it is no less frightful for all that. Words will no longer deceive. It was precisely with nouns like *virtue, beneficence, justice* and *humanity*, that the arch-revolutionary himself [Robespierre] shaped the mechanism of that government in the period of its greatest activity. In vain you would employ even more imposing terms: all that the people would still expect from them would be all the known and unknown ills.[18]

Abuse of power and abuse of words are identical. Babeuf's diagnosis, dictated by his experience of 1793–4, had already been implied by the letter he had written to the Abbé Coupé (in the summer of 1791) on the eve of the elections to the Legislative Assembly. That letter had been both a confession and a profession of faith, and also a self-critical meditation on the function of the elected representative: why do we become a part of power? what desire impels us to do so? and what legitimises that desire itself? With his inner regard for honesty, Babeuf ponders the danger of 'presumptuousness' ('that sort of inner vanity which leads us to believe that we are better than many of our brothers'). Contaminated as it is by the spirit of domination, passion for politics means vainglory, vice and perversion. It becomes a virtue with that person who alone answers the call of the common good. But how do you guarantee that it is virtue? and get it recognised? Here Babeuf can only fall back on Rousseauistic assumptions: the purity of an individual is proved by his transparency. And it is by martyrdom – successive privation and persecution – that he can confirm his vocation as a 'champion of the people'. We once more discover therefore, in Babeuf, what made for the prestige and the exceptionality of Jean-Jacques Rousseau who, though never quoted, is constantly present. But also that is precisely what gives force to this laicised version of Christian discourse which speaks out against the spirit of domination and its expedients: secrecy, ruse and double-talk. . . . whether the person on trial is the 'tyrant Robespierre' or whether it is the torturers like Carrier whose desire came down to the 'quite extraordinary frenzy for unlimited domination'.[19] Faced with all the blood spilled throughout History, Babeuf wishes to remain pure. But how do you interpret the exercise of power and political responsibility if you confine yourself to a morality of conviction? Babeuf's answer to this conundrum is headlong flight into prophetic militantism

Apostolate and prophecy: the emergence of the tribune

From the outset, Babeuf organised his self-presentation in such a way as to intensify the traits of his uncommon identity. The diversity of the rôles he plays is translated by the diversity of the expressive registers he uses and by a style which covers the whole range of pronouns. In the petition and the address, the 'nous' of the enunciator clearly shows the oneness of a collective subject. When the militant is faced with calumny, he responds by using a polemical third person: 'Babeuf est-il un factieux?' (Is Babeuf seditious?). Then there is the ironic 'je' of the private letter ('Je fis mon petit heros': I acted the little hero) which alternates with the emphatic 'je' of the unrecognised pioneer who underlines his own qualities.[20] In short, the apology for self combines the *topoi* of the 'plaidoyer *pro domo*' (plea in self-defence) with the eloquence of the eulogy. Babeuf's figure as apostle and prophet is constructed with the rhetoric of the self-portrait.

As early as April 1787, the author of the *Cadastre perpétuel* had prided himself on 'suffering in the person of his brothers', on transmitting 'the massed cry of suffering humanity'.[21] In 1791, his plea for the peasants of Davenécourt is embellished with a splendid anti-feudal prophecy taken from Raynal and, thus magnified, their conflict assumes significance for the nation, for the world even.[22] From the time he was first put in prison (May–July 1790), Babeuf was hailed as the 'apostle and martyr of the good cause'. He was unemployed, poverty-stricken, the protegé of no one, but persecution turned these marks of disfavour into so many glorious stigmata. Moreover, since he owed his liberation to 'l'Ami du peuple', the prestige of the mediator transformed his misadventure into a blazing ordeal by fire: 'Marat was my defender. His pen of fire brought me purified out of that first great test.'[23]

Related after the event, the skirmishes of 1789–91 take on the radiance of a destiny and the coherence of a vocation. But, in the heat of the moment, the publicist deliberately redefines an identity for himself, which becomes more and more broadly based: in April–May 1790, he modestly signs himself 'citizen soldier at Roye in Picardy'; come the summer, he baptises himself 'the Marat of the department', then the Marat 'of Picardy'; at the end of the year, he is the 'democratic gazeteer'. The drafter of petitions gives way to the editor of an ephemeral *Journal de la Confédération*, and then of a *Correspondant picard*. His name is created by action and symbolises a mission. His authority as a militant (won in Picardy) initially gives substance to his signature. But his legitimacy as a journalist depends essentially on his reputation as a political writer, on the prestige that public opinion bestows on him.

This doubtless explains the gap between his private writings and his public text. In private, he falls prey to megalomania; writing to his wife, he proclaims himself 'the Saviour of mankind'. At the end of 1790, Babeuf is already laying claim to the title of tribune,[24] although he takes care not to profess as much in public. For, if his early ambition is to exercise a sort of tribunate over public opinion, this modest plebeian needs mediators to legitimise that ambition, not least in his own eyes. On 20 August 1791, Francois-Noël-Camille Babeuf confesses to Coupé, his 'brother within the City', that he hesitates to recognise himself in the role of a revolutionary intellectual.[25] And, on 7 May 1793, he addresses to his patron, Chaumette, an elated letter which is a mixture of emulation, challenge and obsequiousness. Babeuf awards to this 'exemplary sans-culotte' (who is destined by his ancient forename for a glorious fate) the title of 'Tribun du Peuple'.[26] Emblematic of devotion to civic duty, the ancient pseudonym confers a sacrificial sovereignty which is the prerogative of the martyr, but – foremost – of the prophet.

We can here define the prophet according to four functions: he addresses his word to the people, to humanity; he speaks in the name of the Other (God) or of others (man); he denounces the ills of the present and discloses the secrets of the past; and, finally, he announces what will be. Babeuf does not publicly adopt this rôle as prophet until late 1794. But his vocation is clearly visible in a whole series of millenarian pronouncements which betray the same impatience to deliver History of its fruits . . . whether we are talking about his attempt, in 1787, to win over his editor ('this is the most favourable moment in a thousand years to show what a plan of this sort is worth') or, in 1795, to utter the great messianic promise ('Let us come, after a thousand years, and change these crude laws').[27]

At the end of November 1793, Babeuf imagines writing an *Histoire nouvelle de Jésus-Christ*,[28] meant for a 'plebeian' public. Never more than a rough draft, this text starts off with an iconoclastic act: the imposture of the false god who sought only to become King of the Jews must be denounced: 'Let there be light [...] I come to tear off the blindfold [...] I attack without mercy the very person of the idol in chief'. The prospectus signed: *Gracchus Babeuf*, articulates the thesis: 'religious mania is mere charlatanism', while an alexandrine: 'Je viens, après mille ans, démasquer ce Dieu-roi' gives emphasis to the apocalyptic act of the prophet (I come, after a thousand years, to unmask this God-king). With his intransigence, Babeuf ties in with the most radical current in the dechristianisation movement and refuses to envisage any theistic or deistic compromise.[29] It is this initial, basic act of sacrilege which allows him to articulate a prophetic discourse. Contrary to Rousseau and his disciples, contrary even to the Hébertist theme of the 'sans-culotte Jesus', Babeuf's atheism rejects the cult of the Supreme Being (by anticipation) and all the christic reasons for justifying it that the Jacobin Republic could possibly seek.[30] And his style of writing? Although it had been accidental and parodical in 1791, his pastiche of biblical style becomes the essential force behind his own style in 1795–6. For, if Babeuf secularises the figure of Jesus to the point of denying his divinity, it is definitely because he needs to clear the decks for an inverse strategy of sacralisation which will messianise the Cause of the Equals and raise 'plebeianism' to the status of a new Gospel.[31]

On 5 October 1794, number 23 of Babeuf's paper opens with two surprises: 'I am changing titles': no longer is it *Le Journal de la liberté de la presse* but *Le Tribun du Peuple* (hereafter *Tribun*) and 'I shall also justify my first name': now Gracchus and no longer Camille. These mutations solemnly announce the public birth of the Tribune.

Concerning the deliberate choice of his successive forenames, Babeuf explained himself all the more freely since each one symbolised a turning point in his life as an individual, as a citizen and as a militant. In November 1790, at Roye, he made 'public abjuration of Catholicism' and replaced Francois-Noël by: Camille (emblem of civil peace, and of the reconciliation between patricians and plebeians). But it was only in September 1794 that Camille became his signature as a journalist, harmonising with the Thermidorian (i.e. civil concord) line of his *Journal de la liberté de la presse*. Conversely, when Babeuf adopted Gracchus as his first name, it was because the mood of the time was for war and because one had to display a combative identity. The signature Gracchus Babeuf was first used in May 1793 in private writings which showed the inspiration of a Chaumette type of Cordelier sans-culottism. But it was between 5–13 October 1794 (*Tribun*, nos. 23–27) that the new Gracchus suddenly appears on the public scene, making a sensational – and yet ambiguous – entrance because he remains a left-wing Thermidorian who is fighting for the rebirth of the popular societies crushed by the Terror. Babeuf's arrest and the closing of the clubs remove the ambiguity. Then the Tribune can fully gauge the risks to which he is committed by the austerity of the name of the Gracchi. By contrast with Christian forenames, ancient-style names (chosen precisely for their energetic and sacrificial value) connote heroic mobilisation and a willingness – in the fight – to accept martyrdom.[32]

At the beginning of issue number 23, Babeuf analyses the two components of the term 'People's Tribune'. Were it not for the usurpers, the first component would be self-evident: 'any and every newspaper title should display the sacred name of the people'. Unlike the usurped titles with which the false 'friends' or 'orators' of the people adorn themselves, Babeuf's own status as a tribune is guaranteed by the authenticity of his 'plebeianism'. Nevertheless, when he uses the title of 'Tribune', it oscillates between a minimal and a maximal meaning. On the one hand, his function as orator and publicist is far removed from the Roman tribunate. For lack of a solidly founded right of objection, it is precariousness that characterises this 'purely moral magistrature' which remains an unmandated power of opinion. But at other times – particularly in the *Manifeste* – the notion is at its broadest and most prestigious because, designating them as the 'most distinguished tribunes' – Babeuf brings together in one single Pantheon a glorious cohort of legislators and philosophers: side by side together, we find Lycurgus the founder, Jean-Jacques (summed up in one maxim from the *Contrat Social*), Morelly masquerading as Diderot (taken to be the author of the *Code de la nature*), Robespierre for his Declaration of Rights, and finally Saint-Just who is credited with a fine line on the unfortunate who are 'the powerful of the earth'.

From prophecy to martyrdom: the messianic utterance

Unlike the *Philosophes*, who always violently denigrated the prophetic function, the direct descendants of the Enlightenment (particularly in the period 1789–96) happily claimed to be apostles of Reason. Coming after Fauchet, Marat and Jacques Roux, Babeuf is also an eloquent representative of this revolutionary recurrence of prophetism. Starting in December 1794 (*Tribun*, no. 24), prophetic articulation allows him to present himself as the leader of a 'plebeian party' in gestation. The criticism that he makes of his recent Thermidorian past is shrouded in a messianic enthusiasm which is both ingenuous and immodest: 'I seize once again the thunderbolt of truth [...] I become myself again; I forswear all pretence' (*incipit* of no.

28). This concern for speaking true gives an edge to his satire of Thermidorian turpitudes: we find him vituperating, with sarcastic aggressiveness (no. 28), against 'l'empire de la frisure' (the domination of the curly locks) and 'la législation de la perruque' (the legislation of the periwig) before he goes on to make an attack on Mme Tallien and the other 'Venus- Dubarrys' (no. 29). This art of vengeful vociferation, which Marat used to call 'raising the roof', has been appropriated by Babeuf: 'In this issue, the People's Tribune is putting in the windows and letting out all the important truths' (no. 29). This he can do because his break with Thermidor allows him once more to be blunt. When he speaks, it will henceforth be from the depths of a 'vault' (like Marat), from on high in a 'garret' (like the plebeian thinker), or from within a 'workshop' (like a Parisian artisan). Across working-class Paris, the flame of a free press kindles 'a hundred thousand living lights': 'each hovel, each garret is now a club' (no. 31).

Babeuf's prophetic transports mark him out as the leader of a chosen people. As such, he 'reveals' the division of France into two camps: in the one, 'the bogus people', 'the gilded millions', in the other, 'the real people', the 'twenty four million empty stomachs'. To be able to combat that rich enemy designated as 'them', the 'me' and the 'you' must be fused together into the conflictual 'we' of an organisable plebeian party. This manichean stance (seen for the first time in no. 29) serves as the analysis for the current situation and the legitimisation of an ancestral struggle: 'the war of those who have nothing against those who have everything' (no. 40). The analysis is, of course, blind to the real respective strengths of the adversaries. But it *is* a mobilising incantation for those who are deepest in despair. It is that precise tension which makes for the power of Babeuf's prophetism: on the one hand there is the discourse of a political leader with his programme, but on the other an eschatological discourse which has neither time set for delivery nor common assent. One year later, the Conspiracy of the Equals will live and *die* because of that cleavage.

Between the appearance of nos. 32 and 34 of the *Tribun* (i.e. February–November 1795), Babeuf spends nine months in prison, in that melting pot in which the heterogeneous elements of the future Conspiracy were to join forces. What makes him stand out in that alliance is the sheer energy of his style which, in the last issues of the *Tribun* (November 1795–April 1796), takes the written word into the realm of the hypnotic state. Babeuf, like Marat, ascribes this feverish rhetoric to a legitimate frenzy, to that fusional enthusiasm for the struggle to ensure 'collective happiness'. At the trial in Vendôme, Pillé, his secretary, will recount the unbridled gesticulating of the writer Babeuf: 'I say in all good faith, I have seen Babeuf quite ill, running about his bedroom, jumping up and down saying: We are in a state of insurrection!'

Babeuf, as the person concerned, confirms this statement, seeing in these paroxysms but the symptoms of the authentic revolutionary 'malady': 'When I was composing an issue of the *Tribun* [...], I would warm to my task and would cudgel my brains. I think that this is a fairly common habit among those who write'.[33]

If we wish to get a living impression of one of those feverish, creative crises, we can read, as a free-standing entity, issue no. 34 which opens with his prospectus, and issue no. 35 which culminates in the famous *Manifeste des plébéiens*. . . in other words, more than one hundred and fifty pages of torrential utterance. Basing himself on a two-fold assumption: 'the goal of society is collective happiness/the people struggle for collective happiness', Babeuf (in his prospectus) defines 'the tribunic task' as being 'a new evangelisation' and the respective camps are indicated by the polemical and messianic way in which Babeuf choreographs the struggle. In a seething mass of vengeful exclamations, the enemy is referred to by way of three pronouns: 'you' means the tyrants; 'they' the 'gilded people'; 'them' (eux) the bribe-taking publicists. The 'I' is no longer the 'I' of a journalist addressing his readers (though it was so down to no. 28), it is the 'I' of a plebeian leader signing a permanent pact with his people. The latter bring him their strength and, in exchange, 'the apostle' or 'the Hercules' of the 'true people' will point to the land promised to the 'Friends and Brothers' (no. 34).

Babeuf's strictly political discourse remains vague. Until an 'insurrectional declaration' can be made, the only strategic imperative that he can give concerns the creation of a rebel centre called (in a particularly ambivalent marriage of terms) either 'a plebeian Vendée' or – by reference to Rome and to Year II – 'the Sacred Mount' or 'the plebeian Mountain'. But, not being very politically aware, and being even less a statesman, Babeuf prophesies unreservedly. Amalgamating the tone of the pamphlet with the pastiche of the Bible, his abuse either goes from picturesque uses of sarcasm to hallucinated expressions of anathema, or it visualizes, in one breathless tableau, the effects of the 'Thermidorian derevolution'. Sometimes the prophet takes fright at his own visions, admitting to the 'excessive audaciousity (*audacieuseté*) of [his] independent pen' (no. 34). But, in no. 35, these doubts become less frequent and give way to admonition, to preaching, to an irresistible messianic scheme of utterance which grows drunk on its own extraordinary enthusiasm.

Though time will not allow a close analysis of his rhetoric in the *Manifeste*, we should however note that Babeuf builds up his persona and gives it real substance by five different argumentative processes. The first two valorise his political vigilance: writing on 30 November 1795, the 'athlete' of free opinion denounces a servile press and makes himself – with tones of deep emotion – the spokesman for the 'women of Paris' who, in distress, are crying out their hunger. The next three processes uncouple the discourse from any reference to current events: first, making a leap back into a founding past, Babeuf takes his place in the Pantheon of the great tribunes (see p. 86); then, making a leap forward into the hoped-for future, he sees himself scaling the plebeian Mountain there to pen 'the Decalogue of holy humanity'; and finally, he stands aloof from the religion of the Prophets which he repudiates because: 'all that inspires the republican divinities is manifest in all simplicity, under the auspices of nature (God supreme) through the voice speaking from the heart of republicans' (no. 35). Then come the ten pages of the great *Manifeste* which are better read, less as the methodical exposé of a body of doctrine, than as the tumultuous ephiphany of the principles of Equality. The prophet pretends to efface himself behind his people ('Let the people proclaim their Manifesto'), but this is in order to give voice to a solemn 'we'. Every precept of this 'code of nature' obtrudes as an indisputable judgement, as a necessary truth the proof of which will be furnished by future time: 'We shall explain/we shall define/we shall demonstrate', etc. His teaching places us face to face ultimately with a vast oratorical movement in which we find an ultimate recapitulation and peroration, along with an imprecation against 'tyrants', the whole thing culminating in the vehemence of an apocalyptic cry:

> All our sufferings are at their peak [...] Let everything return to chaos, and from chaos let there come a new and regenerated world! LET US COME, AFTER A THOUSAND YEARS, AND CHANGE THESE CRUDE LAWS.

From November 1795 to April 1796 (nos. 35–43), the Conspiracy still has five months in which to develop its propaganda and to create for itself the traps in which the Directory will ensnare it. The bible of the movement remains Babeuf's *Manifeste*, whereas Maréchal's *Manifeste des Egaux* gives cause for disagreement. The two texts diverge doctrinally, but if we relate them to the current situation (i.e. the way in which this insurgent minority was isolated, had been infiltrated, etc.), we can see Babeuf and Maréchal engaged in the same headlong flight into a type of messianism in which utopia and insurgency become entwined: 'Torn between a dead past and an imaginary future', the Equals are definitely 'men without a present'.[34]

These contradictions find their rhetorical expression in the *Tribun*: the imperatives of the Secret Directory are mitigated into calls (both vehement and vague) to participate in an ever-imminent uprising. Enraged and incantatory, this paralysis is expressed in different ways:– for example, the enunciator speaks less to the militants than to a universal audience, to a tribunal formed by posterity. Is this the prudence of the conspirator or the strategy of despair? At any rate when, finally, in mid-April 1797, the time for repression comes, there runs through the final issue of the *Tribun* (no.

43) a sort of heroic relief: 'All is fulfilled. Terror against the People is the order of the day [...] Friends! All this is nothing. I command that you remain energetic [...] Liberty in France is immortal.'

The same hope had animated the martyrs of Prairial (May 1795). But those victims of the cowardice of political schemers had refused to sanction revenge, as they had refused to sanction any plan for an insurrection, from fear of a renewed Terror.[35] How do you disengage from a state of Terror without destroying the Republic? Benjamin Constant answered this question in May 1796, pleading for a Republic which is capable of arbitrating the conflict of interests out of respect for the principles of 89.[36] In the name of the constitution of 93, the Conspiracy of the Equals gives the inverse answer: get civil society admitted into the paradise of collective happiness by means of a violent catastrophe which makes political mediation redundant. This strategic void is again apparent in Babeuf's system of defence in Vendôme: deny the plannned insurgency, celebrate the cult of Equality, offer to be the expiatory victim. Hence the great, five-day ceremonial of the *Défense Générale* which celebrates that sacrifice. . . freely-consented even unto death, and which consecrates the father and founding martyr elevating his own statue in a sort of funeral oration which is a mixture of tenderness and despair, serenity and intoxication.

The clearest sign of these *ultima verba* lies perhaps, as early as 14 July 1796, in a letter to Le Peletier in which Babeuf leaves as inheritance his heart, his written word, his legend, 'all that the corrupt people of today call my dreams'.

In today's world, Babeuf is being set free from that reductive genealogy which formerly made of him the necessary precursor of a regimented collectivism.[38] His text – disparate, pleonastic, highly individualistic and bearing a powerful message – has started to invite other types of analysis which are rhetorical in nature. Babeuf the apostle has his niche in a history of revolutionary oracular pronouncements with their romantic, socialist and anarchistic repercussions. As a militant for equality of rights, Babeuf can help us to understand the novel conjunction – during the Revolution – between ethics and politics, literature and democracy. Liberated from sectarian fetishism, Babeuf can at last find his place among 'those writers of the people' whose 'great secret' was admired by Baudelaire in 1851 when he called their ardour, their faith, their joy: that 'goût infini de la République'.[39]

NOTES

1 When translated into English, Babeuf's 'bonheur commun' is unfailingly rendered as 'common happiness'. This literal translation strikes me as being too neutral a way of doing justice to what is, after all, for Babeuf a talisman-phrase with invariably powerful poetic/political reverberations. Given that his 'bonheur *commun*' is to be an all-embracing, communal experience, the perpetually renovated result of the united efforts of the totality (as strictly opposed to, and quite distinct from, individuals), it seems that we should be looking for a word which conveys the sense of mankind's being at once both patient and agent. In one sense, we are looking at an almost classic definition of the word *collective*. 'Collective happiness' is, in my opinion, precisely the phrase which makes for an appropriate, emotionally charged translation... although I am not unaware that certain social and political considerations may tend to make it too charged in one specific direction. But translation often does tend to mean replacing one problem with another [Ed.].

2 Jules Michelet, *Histoire du XIXe siècle*, in *Oeuvres complètes*, vol. XXI, ed. Paul Viallaneix, Flammarion, 1982, p. 347. See also Paul Viallaneix, *La voie royale. Essai sur l'idee de peuple dans l'oeuvre de Michelet*, Paris, 1959, pp. 398–406 (on Michelet and Babeuf).

3 See Valentin Jamerey-Duval, *Mémoires. Enfance et éducation d'un paysan au XVIIIe siècle*, ed. J. M. Goulemot, Le Sycomore, 1981; *Pierre Prion scribe*, ed. E. Le Roy Ladurie and O. Ranum, Archives, Gallimard Julliard, 1985; Jacques-Louis Ménétra, *Journal de ma vie*, ed. D. Roche, Montalba, 1982.

4 With the exception of one article dated 10 November 1790, the forty issues of the *Le Correspondant picard* have still not been found. For that article, see Babeuf, *Ecrits*, ed. C. Mazauric, Messidor Editions Sociales, 1988, pp. 187–92.

5 R. Andrews, 'Réflexions sur la Conjuration des Egaux', *Annales, ESC*, janvier-février 1974, pp. 73–106.

6 G. Benrekassa, 'Camille Desmoulins, écrivain révolutionnaire: Le Vieux Cordelier', in *La Carmagnole*, pp. 223–41.

7 Ph. Roger, 'L'homme de sang: l'invention sémiotique de Marat', in *La Mort de Marat*, pp. 141–66.

8 W. G. Hegel, *La Phénoménologie de l'Esprit* (French trans.), Aubier, vol. I, p. 309.

9 Babeuf, *Oeuvres*, ed. V. Dalin, A. Saïtta and A. Soboul, P., Commission d'histoire économique et sociale de la Révolution française, 1977, vol. I, p. 341. Letter to his son Robert, dated 25 July 1789, in which he describes the feverish atmosphere in Paris.

10 V. Dalin, *Babeuf avant et pendant la Révolution française* (French trans.), 2e édition, 1987, p. 434.

11 Jules Michelet, *Histoire de la Révolution française*, IX, 5, Gallimard, Pléiade, vol. II, pp. 78–9.

12 Babeuf, *Oeuvres*, p. 340.

13 *Le Système de dépopulation* has just been re-edited, with an apocryphal

title – *La Guerre de la Vendée* – and a debatable introduction by S. Secher and J. J. Bregeon (Taillandier, 1987).

14 Michelet, *Histoire du XIXe siècle*, p. 102.

15 On the relationship between Babeuf and Fouché, see R. B. Rose, *Gracchus Babeuf, the First Revolutionary Communist*, Stanford University Press, 1978, pp. 178–9, 187, 208–9.

16 See P. Buonarroti, *Conspiration pour l'égalité, dite de Babeuf*, ed. by G. Lefèbvre and J. Dautry, Editions Sociales, (2 vol.), 1957, vol. II, pp. 164–70.

17 Babeuf, *Journal de la liberté de la presse* (reprint, Paris, EDHIS), no. 2, 5 septembre 1794.

18 Babeuf, *Ecrits*, pp. 228-9.

19 Babeuf, *Systeme de dépopulation* (edition quoted), p. 82.

20 'I disclosed the dreadful mysteries surrounding the encroachments of the noble class, I unveiled them to the people through fiery texts published at the very beginning of the revolution', in Dalin, *Babeuf*, p. 199 (letter to Devin, 10 May 1790) and pp. 302–3 (letter to Sylvain Maréchal, March 1793).

21 Babeuf, *Oeuvres*, p. 363.

22 Dalin, *Babeuf*, pp. 324–5.

23 *Ibid*, p. 212 and p. 242 (letter to Menessier, 1793).

24 'I have been raised up by the people as a new tribune' (letter to the *curé* of Longueval), *ibid.*, p. 243.

25 'I do not know whether I am mistaken, but I have the impression that the Revolution has spoiled me dreadfully; I often find myself thinking that I have become quite unsuited for any type of employment other than publicism [...]. I incline to think that this is my unique vocation', *ibid.*, p. 341.

26 'Come, you are our legislator [...]. It is your own commitment, Anaxagoras the tribune, that I am calling upon you to fulfil.', *Ecrits*, pp. 209–11.

27 *Le Tribun du peuple* (reprint, Paris, EDHIS), no. 35, 30 novembre 1795, *Manifeste des plébéiens*. See also *Ecrits*, p. 281. For the letter to his editor, see Dalin, *Babeuf*, p. 128.

28 Dalin, *Babeuf*, pp. 473–4 for the totality of the quotations drawn from that rough draft.

29 His position will remain unchanged down to the *Manifeste des plébéiens* (30 November 1795) and will not shift until the trial in Vendôme when he moves closer to his companions, in particular to Germain who was a fervent follower of the 'egalitarian Jesus'.

30 See D. Menozzi, *Les interprétations politiques de Jésus, de l'Ancien Régime à la Révolution* (French trans.), Editions du Cerf, 1983, in particular pp. 213, 226, 235, 246–7.

31 See Dalin, *Babeuf*, p. 325: satirical pastiche of the biblical text in a letter to 'dame Lemire'.

32 'We have sent to the scaffold our Camilles, our Anaxagorases, our Anarcharsises; but I am not intimidated by any of that' (*Le Tribun du Peuple*, no. 23, 5 octobre 1794). See also *Ecrits*, p. 224.

33 Quoted by M. Dommanget, *Sur Babeuf et la conspiration des Egaux*, Maspero, 1970, pp. 25–6.
34 R. Andrews, 'Réflexions sur la Conjuration des Egaux', p. 105.
35 See, in the proceedings of the Clermont and Riom colloquium: *Gilbert Romme et son temps*, PUF, 1966 (2e partie, 'sur le suicide heroique'), the article of J. Dautry, 'Réflexions sur les martyrs de Prairial', p. 201.
36 *De la force du gouvernement actuel de la France et de la nécessité de s'y rallier,* réédition Champs, Flammarion, 1988.
37 The text of the admirable letter to Le Peletier is in *Pages choisies* ed. M. Dommanget, Colin, 1935, pp. 318–9.
38 We have another recent example of this authoritarian type of History (Babeuf is one of its victims) in A. Ioanissian's *Les Idées communistes pendant la Révolution française* (French trans.), Moscou, Editions du Progrès, 1986.
39 Baudelaire, 'Pierre Dupont, I', in *Oeuvres complètes*, Gallimard, Pléiade, vol. II, p. 33.

ROUND-TABLE DISCUSSION

Opening the discussion, Philippe ROGER asked whether some clarification could be given regarding the role of 'examen de conscience' (self-examination/deliberate introspection) in the work of Babeuf. It seemed that this could be an important aspect of his literary strategies because Eric Walter had alluded to the fact that Babeuf had often been dependent, manipulated, hired. Given that particular background, in what manner did his 'discours de la transparence' and his self-affirmation express themselves? Did he talk about this problem? Did he depict it?
Eric WALTER: 'I have been looking at Babeuf from the biographical angle; as always, it has been difficult to distinguish the psychological from the rhetorical. But my answer would be that, if there are no *overt* traces in Babeuf's texts of any awareness of a contradiction between an ideal of revolutionary purity and the compromises that life forces upon us, the only indications of self-examination that you can find are in letters mostly to his wife. Let me quote you a letter of 27 May 1793; Babeuf has recently been employed at the 'Commission des Subsistances' (Board of Food) and here is how he talks about his promotion: "Here I have for friends the most distinguished people in Paris: Chaumette, the Prosecutor of the Commune; Pache, the mayor; Garin [municipal officers and general administrators of the Board of Food]; Robespierre; Sylvain Maréchal, the editor of the *Révolutions de Paris*, and many others. All these people make me, with my poor accoutrements, most kindly welcome. A good dinner is waiting for me when I go to see them. In the days that follow I eat just bread. This change from one extreme to the other makes no impression on me. You will no doubt have little trouble in believing this, for you know that I customarily go from good to ill-fortune with the greatest indifference" [Dalin, *Babeuf*, p.436].'

Alain BOURDON, alluding to the figure of Marat as politician, journalist and prophet, wondered whether Babeuf's conduct and exploits had in any way been influenced by, or imitated from, 'L'Ami du Peuple'? Eric WALTER admitted that, in preparing his paper, he had been brought to angle his presentation along the lines of Philippe Roger's earlier piece entitled 'L'homme de sang: l'invention semiotique de Marat' [in *la Mort de Marat*, pp. 141–66]. 'Many of the elements found in Marat's projection of himself are also to be discerned in Babeuf, but *minus* one: minus the idea of the bloody sacrifice of his own person. With him, in the years 1789–1796, there is no *explicit* statement that *his* blood , or that of others, will be connected with "puissances obscures" (occult powers), although there is a trace of this in his text on the Vendée [*Système de dépopulation*] when he says that –in the blood of the executed –there are forces which are both good and bad, and which ultimately bring about these situations of Terror. But Babeuf himself never demanded or wanted the Terror as such, quite unlike Marat who, as early as 31 May –2 June 1793, settles into a system of Terror, and whose strength therein came from the fact that not only did he offer his own blood and life but also make of this invocation to blood the vector of his rhetoric.'

Peter FRANCE, taking the parallel further, asked what relationship could be discerned between the written, journalistic word and the spoken. Which had the greater 'prophetic' force? Could one simultaneously be both prophet and deputy? Eric WALTER: 'That is the whole problem with journalists: their language and their discourse have no immediate sanction. That is the way in which people have tried to define the problem in the case of Marat. They are intellectuals without a mandate who are answerable only to their own consciences (and then to their readers). But it is interesting in the case of Babeuf to see how the textual figure of the reader appears very clearly in September–October 1794, in his *Journal de la liberté de la presse*, numbers 1–22, because we are witnessing, in form and content, a struggle precisely for the liberty of the press. He addresses his message to an imprecise reader who is nevertheless expected to "take" the discourse "on board". On the other hand, however, in *Le Tribun du Peuple* the textual figure of the reader slowly disappears and it is "le peuple elu" (the chosen people) who become his target, the other half of the dialogue'. Peter FRANCE: 'I discern here a reversal of roles between prophet and speaker *vis-a-vis* this *Word of Fire* which fires the people. In these conditions the speaker/orator is subject to certain constraints in the Assembly, whereas the real liberty belongs to the writer. If you compare the texts that Marat wrote with those he "spoke", you can see greater liberty in *L'Ami du Peuple*. He puts me in mind of Rousseau who said: "To write and remain hidden is precisely what suits me best" [*Confessions*, Book III].' Eric WALTER: 'Rousseau's statement is highly applicable to Marat who had to contend with the problem of what he called "his new court". In fact Michelet claimed that Marat was dead politically from the time of his election to the Convention. But to come back to Babeuf and to the relationship between the written word and the spoken word, Babeuf is really no different from anyone else: preparing to speak publicly in the district of Montdidier or to take up arms for the peasants [1790–1], he –the "Marat of the Somme" *–writes out* his speeches (and these speeches show that he was capable of very great variations in his discourse). But you gain the strong impression that what he wrote was meant to be read aloud by others in an assembly or in a group of people, and read in the sense specifically that his word was to be retransmitted by being spoken aloud'. Peter FRANCE: 'That raises another aspect of Babeuf's rhetoric. Since rhetoric presupposes a relationship between a speaker and a listener (even if the "speaker", in the instance you quote, is an intermediary for the real speaker), I should like to know something about the immediate reactions of a reading/listening public. Marat, for example, was read and was influential; there was a clear two-way current. With Babeuf, it does not seem so evident. Was he speaking to keep his courage up (whistling in the dark) rather than trying to establish real communication with an audience?' Eric WALTER said that a good idea of the precise relationship could in fact be gained because, in his *Journal de la liberté de la presse*, Babeuf had published his readers' letters. 'Let me quote from issue number 40, that is to say 24 February 1796. This is a letter from the "département du Mont Blanc": "Equality, virtue, liberty. It is given but to you o Gracchus! to pronounce these great truths which strike terror" (they write like him!). Or again, from the Pas-de-Calais: "You summon together, o Tribune! in your number 39, page 208 (and they read closely!), all the equals of '92 and commit yourself to edifying all brothers, to encouraging and instructing them for the greatest progress of propogandism which is a sacred dogma, to filling all enemies with dread [...]. We are sending you for inclusion in the annals of truth two printed pieces which will prove to you that, in Year II of the Republic, your religion was already known among us". These letters indicate that there *was* a type of feed-back and that Babeuf's impact on his public can doubtless be measured by them; but that correspondence has yet to be exploited properly.'

Joanna KITCHIN took up the reference to Babeuf's subscribers and asked whether they were numerous and whether there was reasonably detailed information about them; who they were and where they lived. Eric WALTER replied that the extant Babeuf papers (which were largely in Moscow) gave a good idea of his reading public. A certain amount of work had been done on the topic and was readily accessible [A. Mathiez, *Revue des Cours et Conférences*, 1928–9, pp.559 ff.; A. Soboul, 'Personnel sectionnaire et personnel babouviste' in *Babeuf et les problèmes du Babouvisme* (Colloque international de Stockholm, 21 août 1960), Editions Sociales, 1963, pp. 107–31].

Alain BOURDON: 'One gets the impression that Babeuf and Marat create a sort of sacred notion of Republicanism which manifests itself in their rhetoric, in the content of their writings, in their behaviour and even in their theatricality'. Eric WALTER agreed that this was very evident in the case of Babeuf in a variety of ways. 'His first important work, the *Cadastre perpétuel* of 1789, had about it a certain messianic tone, a prophetic fervour which is fairly typical of the late Enlightenment and which puts one in mind of the Abbé Raynal. But I see those traits you mention coming to the fore particularly from the time of his *Manifeste des Plébéiens* onwards [number 35 of the *Tribun du Peuple*, November 1795] when it becomes clear that Babeuf is constructing a sectarian discourse. One should look closely at his modes of address, at his interpellations, for example: "equals", "brothers and friends", "the holy league united by the sacred dogma". The formula however which predominates by far is "brothers and friends". I should mention also that this vocabulary, and other similar vocabulary in Babeuf, has been seen as masonic'. In response to a query from Siân REYNOLDS (who wanted to know how soon the formula *salut et fraternité* –which was used in the Paris Commune of 1871 in deliberate reference to the Revolution –had been used to round off correspondence), both Eric WALTER and Philippe ROGER joined in explaining that the word *fraternity* as such had appeared very early in the epistolary rites of the lodges (as it had in the revolutionary political societies). The real problem with such formulae, like *salut et fraternité*; *liberté, égalité, fraternité*, is however to know when they are in settled or institutionalised usage, or accepted as a part of coded rhetoric. *Fraternité* was definitely masonic. Aulard had moreover suggested that this particular word married all the more easily with the word *liberté*, and above all with *égalité*, since the idea of equality is present in practically all masonic forms of address. The majority of masonic correspondence from before the Revolution starts with: 'I write to you from a place of peace and equality'... the place being the lodge. Philippe ROGER: 'When you are talking about fraternity, I think that you must distinguish between *fusional* fraternity (for example the *Fête de la Fédération*) and fraternity through Terror. Babeuf can be talked about only in terms of the first. There is, of course, a possible rather curious link between Babeuf and his masonic-sounding vocubulary and the *Cercle social*, a revolutionary group with strong masonic affiliations, the leading spirits of which were the Abbé Claude Fauchet and the journalist Nicolas de Bonneville (whose first newspaper was incidentally entitled *Le Tribun du Peuple*!) We know that Babeuf went to the *Cercle social* in December 1790, considered himself for a time an adherent as we know that it was Claude Fauchet who massively introduced the whole vocabulary of fraternity'. Eric WALTER: 'With Babeuf you meet increasingly often a synonym for "brothers"; that word is, of course, the "Equals". "Brothers", with Babeuf, is an interpellative figure used to designate those who are jointly engaged in an action which may be called sacrificial. "Equals" is both what they are potentially and what they will really be once society has been reorganised along the lines of "holy equality".'

Alain BOURDON, taking up a further problem of vocabulary, sought clarification as to why Babeuf should have called himself 'Le Tribun du Peuple'; had Babeuf seen a parallel between his attributes and those of a Roman tribune? Philippe ROGER wondered also whether that parallel was not there, because it seemed to link up with the demands made at that time for a war leader. Marat, for example, had been demanding such a leader for almost two years. Eric WALTER said that the ultimate insurrection [La Conspiration des Egaux of April-May 1796] with which Babeuf had been so prominently associated might lead one to believe so. But, in reality, their respective positions had been incompatible. Marat had indeed wanted a *military* tribune; as he had said [*Ami du peuple*, no. 173, 26 January 1790]: 'If I were the people's tribune and supported by several thousand determined men, I guarantee after six weeks that the constitution would be perfect [...] '. For Babeuf, that would immediately have raised the whole problem of violence (which I have already talked about at length). His own definition [7 may 1794] was much simpler :'I give this title no more latitude than to fittingly qualify a true defender of *sans-culotterie*' [*Ecrits*, 'Lettre à Anaxagoras Chaumette', p. 207 n.3]'

Nelly WILSON: 'Going back to the notions of liberty and equality, I wonder whether Babeuf's originality is not to be seen in the influence which he exercised over the libertarians, at the end of the century and onwards; the latter had seen a rather complex relationship between liberty and equality. Babeuf's notion of equality is not equality before the law but rather that social and socio-economic equality that was much appreciated by both them and the Socialists'. Eric WALTER intervened to say that such an interpretation was shared by R.B. Rose [*Gracchus Babeuf, the First Revolutionary Communist*, Stanford University Press, 1978] who, far from seeing Babeuf as a pioneer of the doctrine of the revolutionary dictatorship of an elite, had defended the thesis that his importance lay in his contribution to the development of the theory and tactics of a widely based and even libertarian democracy. Nelly WILSON referred back to an earlier exchange initiated by Peter

France [p. 94] on the prophetic quality of Babeuf's utterances. 'I believe that his notion of equality, and his preoccupation with social matters, is linked with the notion of the prophetic spirit. We have a tendency to judge the prophetic spirit, hence the prophet himself, as someone who *predicts*. But it is just as possible to see the biblical prophet, for instance, as someone who *sees* the present ills. If he foresees or predicts, then he predicts catastrophes because nothing is being done to counter the present ills. There is an extremely strong social note with the prophets, as there is with many Socialists'. Philippe ROGER was not convinced that Babeuf was particularly original in this respect. 'Marat is totally similar. With him what you emphatically have is self-proclamation as a prophet who sees things which are *there*. He is the prophet of denunciation. He completely adopts the prophet's ways, calling himself either a prophet or the *Cassandra of the Revolution*. As for the themes of equalilty, and not just of civil equality, they are already in Book II, chapter xi of the *Contrat Social*, where Rousseau says: "Should we inquire in what consists the greatest good of all, which must be the aim of every system of legislation, we shall find that it can be reduced to two main heads: *liberty* and *equality*." He then devotes a paragraph to saying that he is talking about uniformity of conditions: "I have already described the nature of civil liberty. I turn now to equality. Let it be clearly understood that, in using the word, I do not mean that power and wealth must be absolutely the same for all, but only that power should need no sanction of violence but be exercised solely by virtue of rank and legality, while wealth should never be so great that a man can buy his neighbour, nor so lacking that a man is compelled to sell himself". So Rousseau is already making a claim for social equality, but not civil equality. I see Babeuf as being very much in the rousseauistic line'. Nelly WILSON did not see that consideration as detracting from Babeuf's status as a revolutionary thinker, if only by virtue of the fact that he was envisaging an agrarian and not an industrial community. Eric WALTER, following up Philippe Roger's reference to the *Contrat Social*, quoted Babeuf's rather approximate paraphrase of the above development in Book II which he used in his *Manifeste des Plébéiens* when talking about *l'égalité de fait* (equality in fact and practice): 'J. Jacques gave a better definition of this same principle when he wrote: *For the social state to be perfected, each person must have enough*, and no one too much. This short passage is in my opinion the elixir of the social contract. Its author made it as intelligible as he could do at the time he was writing, and few words suffice for him who catches the message' [*Ecrits*, p. 271]. 'This is where there is a meeting of the ways between Jacobin sans-culottism, extreme left-wing Jacobinism and the theory of the Equals. Now as far as the other matter is concerned, the difference between Babeuf and Marat is that Marat is consistently the prophet of *disaster*, a Cassandra for whom there is no future. There is in Marat an extraordinary phrase in which he says that the experience of the fathers can be no use to the sons, because the sons start from zero. Whereas for Babeuf the whole problem was in managing to transmit what was useful to posterity.'

Alain BOURDON: 'In his previous work on Marat, Philippe Roger ['L'homme de sang'] talks about inviolability, a belief in inviolability. Because, as we know, with Marat there is the "ordalie" (ordeal) which serves to prove to himself and to others that he is immune. Is this theme to be found in Babeuf's discourse?' Eric WALTER: 'I have the impression that many people at this time say that they are immune. For example, when Danton says "Je suis impayable" (I am priceless), his is saying more or less the same thing: by a process of trans-substantiation, he is the body of the people or the body of the nation before the Revolutionary Tribunal. And it is this particular notion of immunity – not to be confused with straightforward parliamentary immunity or inviolability – which can be clearly seen with the neo-stoic martyrs of Prairial (Goujon, Romme, Soubrany) who defiantly say: "My body will be taken by what is called justice, but my soul is inviolable and immune from attack". This means that there is an inviolability which is guaranteed by the memory of men. In one word, Diderot's theme of the appeal to posterity has become a very powerful vector force. Returning to Babeuf, we can see that there was in fact self-sacrifice, but *only* at the time of his public trial in Vendôme (February-May 1797). With his temperament (which I have already described for you), with his very theory of discourse, he wanted to put his cards clearly on the table and make a complete declaration. But, in fact, there was an agreement between the Equals that they should shield the great majority and hence save the greatest number of heads. Babeuf had then to deny at all costs the conspiracy aspect, the military organisation of the conspiracy itself, the projected seizure of power. By agreeing to underline the messianic aspect to the exclusion of almost anything else, he doubly sacrificed himself. That is incidentally the reason why, during the trial, his discourse which centred mainly round his "philanthropic dreams" seems "over the top", *délirant* (raving)'.

Approaching a new series of problems, David DENBY suggested that some attention might be given to Babeuf the icon, who is seen by Communists as the precursor of both Communism and Marxism. How much attention had been given to that topic? Eric WALTER: 'There are scholarly works which deal with this problem. R. B. Rose's book [*Gracchus Babeuf*] is absolutely fundamental; then, of course, there is the work of V. M. Dalin [*Babeuf*] which is extremely well documented. I do not believe that there is anything more to be written on Babeuf the ideoloque and founding father of Communism after these two studies in particular. But Dalin, because of the demands of his theoretical position, has to be handled with care. He and other Marxists are sometimes guilty of textual misinterpretations (e.g Babeuf is supposed to have invented the *kolkhozes* in his *Cadastre perpétuel*... which allows Dalin to go even further and claim that Babeuf had already invented not only the communism of distribution but also the communism of production). Generally speaking, the Marxists – who give an idealised portrait of him – are attracted to Babeuf because he is, or can be presented as, a martyr. They can therefore, having claimed him as their own, found a whole tradition and the sacred nature of that tradition in blood. We have nevertheless to be grateful to all these scholars because they have been able to establish that there is no one among the utopian, egalitarian socialists who preceded him (Morelly. Mably, etc) who can compare with Babeuf for the sheer penetration of his economic and social thought. Ten or fifteen years ago, when Babeuf was largely seen as a leveller and not much different from Sylvain Maréchal, I would not have been able to give this paper. But at last the deconstruction of Babeuf is in train.' Joanna KITCHIN, quoting the internationalist ethic of Communism, wanted to know whether Babeuf the precursor had a position *vis-à-vis* international politics and war? Eric WALTER was of the opinion that, although Babeuf's thought was in basis philanthropic and universalist, like all eighteenth-century thought, Babouvism was not in practice truly international. It was not for export (as the Girondins thought the Revolution was for export through war) and certainly made no appeal for 'the workers of the world to unite'. 'I really do have the impression –in the absence of any document proving the contrary – that Babeuf lives in a space which is Picardy, or at the most which is France. Babouvism was nationalistic in temper and visualised no revolutionary action outside France. I suppose, however, that one could claim that he was an internationalist in the same precise sense that eighteenth-century utopians themselves were internationalists: they and he were "internationalists" because they were for humanity reconciled with itself. But, strictly, it was only in the hands of Buonarroti, a generation later, that Babouvism acquired a genuinely international appeal and resonance.'

Replying to David DENBY, who had asked for information about the social content of Babeuf's thought, Eric WALTER admitted that by privileging the prophetic, messianic, possibly eschatological aspect of Babeuf's work, he had not given particular attention to that precise question. It was, however, easy to answer in outline 'Babeuf started as a *feudiste* (a specialist in feudal law and feudal land holdings). He gave great thought to the problem of land distribution and for a time (1790–1), he was a supporter of the famous agrarian law that Claude Fauchet had been preaching. His reading, private study and experience brought him, however, closer and closer to envisaging a rural, communistic community. His communism moreover was strictly agrarian; he had no thoughts on urban revolution, except possibly in the domain of foodstuffs and their distribution. His proposal (1792-93) is for a pooling of land, a communality of production, closely followed by a communality of distribution through communal storehouses which were to share out produce among the Equals. This brought him to make other proposals, for example concerning the status of women, for whom he sought equality (although on a purely political level). In this he was notwithstanding a minority figure because, even among the most democratic of politicians (e.g. Robespierre) anti-feminine prejudice remained strong. He is, however, still dealing with the "women problem" in the last number of the *Tribun du Peuple* (number 43 of 17 April 1796). I suspect that his concern with this issue stems from his notion of what *fraternity* should mean; but it has to be explicable also by his own relationship with his wife which was notable for its high level of liberty and equality. When you consider that Babeuf's whole life, from 1789 to 1796, was totally dominated by politics, you cannot help feeling, by the way, that his wife, who was one of his militant supporters (one of his "co-athletes" as Babeuf would have said), must not only have shared his burning convictions but have also been a most remarkable woman. However, even the acknowledged specialists admit that the domestic details of Babeuf's life, which would be welcome, are mostly lacking'.

Philippe ROGER, drawing together the references to the Equals and to the *Cercle Social* of Fauchet and Bonneville, wondered whether there had been any migration from the latter, after Thermidor, into Babouvist circles. Eric WALTER thought that such a move, born of disillusionment or desperation, was quite possible. 'Certain types of links (though perhaps more apparent than real) do seem to exist. Marcel Dorigny's article ['Le Cercle Social ou les écrivains au cirque', in *La Carmagnole*,, pp. 49–66] should be consulted as also should V.M. Dalin ['Babeuf et le Cercle Social', in *Recherches internationales*, 1970, pp. 62–73]. The trajectory followed by the adherents of the *Cercle* after its dispersal should certainly be examined. I feel sure that the Equals must have recruited from among them, particulary from among those people who, after Thermidor, had not found their place or who were not sufficiently corrupt to feel at ease with the new status quo.'

INDEX